AF657327

INFORMATION SYSTEMS
Global Issues & Emerging Trends

INFORMATION SYSTEMS
Global Issues & Emerging Trends

– Author –
Vinay Chandra
Samir Sinh

Wordpen Academics
Publishing Science That Matter

© 2024 PUBLISHER

Information contained in this work has been published by Wordpen Academics and has been obtained by its author(s)/editor(s) from sources believed to be reliable and are correct to the best of their knowledge. However, the publisher and its author(s) make no representation of warranties with respect of accuracy or completeness of the contents of this book, and shall in no event be liable for any errors, omissions or damages arising out of use of this information and specifically disclaim any implied warranties or merchantability or fitness for any particular purpose.

All rights reserved. Including the right to translate or to reproduce this book or parts thereof except for brief quotations in critical reviews.

ISBN: 978-81-96302-57-3 (Hardback)

Published by : **WORDPEN ACADEMICS**
4736/23, Ansari Road, Darya Ganj,
New Delhi – 110 002
Phone: +91-011-35004336
E-mail: info@wordpenacademics.com

Printed at : **Replika Press Pvt. Ltd.**

Exclusive Distributor: ***Bio-Green Books, New Delhi***

Preface

Information systems are an essential component of modern businesses and organizations, providing critical support for managing processes, data, and decision-making. Information systems can be defined as a combination of hardware, software, data, and procedures used to collect, process, and disseminate information within an organization. It explore the role of information systems in modern organizations, the different types of information systems, and the challenges faced by organizations in managing their information systems. Information systems play a critical role in modern organizations, supporting a wide range of business processes, including accounting, human resources, marketing, supply chain management, and customer service. Information systems provide a platform for managing and organizing data, facilitating communication and collaboration among different departments and teams, and enabling data-driven decision-making. One of the key benefits of information systems is their ability to improve operational efficiency and productivity. By automating routine tasks, streamlining workflows, and reducing manual errors, information systems can help organizations reduce costs, increase efficiency, and improve quality.Another important role of information systems is to support strategic decision-making. By providing accurate and timely data, information systems can help managers and executives make informed decisions about resource allocation, investment opportunities, and long-term planning. Information systems can also provide insights into customer behavior and preferences, enabling organizations to develop more targeted and effective marketing strategies.There are several different types of information systems used in organizations, each designed to support specific business processes and functions. Transaction processing systems (TPS) are used to collect, store, and process data related to day-to-day business transactions, such as sales orders, customer invoices, and inventory updates.Management information systems (MIS) are used to collect and analyze data from various sources to support managerial decision-making.Decision support systems (DSS) are used to provide managers with the tools and information needed to make strategic decisions, often incorporating data from external sources such as market research reports or financial data.Executive support systems (ESS) are designed to provide executives with a high-level view of the organization's performance, incorporating data from various sources to support strategic planning and decision-making.

Despite their benefits, information systems can present significant challenges for organizations. One of the most significant challenges is ensuring the security and confidentiality of data. With the increasing threat of cyber attacks, organizations must invest in robust security measures to protect their data from unauthorized access or theft. Another challenge is the rapid pace of technological change, which can make it difficult for organizations to keep up with the latest developments and maintain their information systems. Organizations must continually invest in training and development programs to ensure that their employees have the skills and knowledge needed to use and manage information systems effectively.Information systems can also present challenges in terms of integration and compatibility. As organizations adopt new technologies and systems, they may need to integrate these with existing systems, which can be time-consuming and expensive. Additionally, different systems may use different data formats or protocols, making it challenging to share data across different platforms. Information systems play a critical role in modern organizations, providing essential support for managing data, processes, and decision-making. Different types of information systems support various business functions, including accounting, marketing, and supply chain management. However, managing information systems can present significant challenges, including security and confidentiality concerns, rapid technological change, and integration and compatibility issues. Organizations must invest in robust security measures, training and development programs, and integration strategies to ensure that their information systems continue to support their business objectives.

Introduces the concept of Information Systems and their importance in modern society. Covers the basic concepts of Information Systems, including data, information, and knowledge, as well as the types of information systems and their components. Explores the use of Bayesian Networks for decision support in emergency response, presenting a model that can be used to aid decision-making in critical situations. Discusses the applicability of Internet Voting in Africa, examining the challenges and opportunities presented by this technology in the context of African countries. It presents a Clinical Pathway for Improving Quality Service and Cost Containment in Hospitals, providing an interdisciplinary approach to healthcare management that combines clinical, managerial, and technological perspectives. This book is highly useful for students of information systems, computer science, and related fields who are interested in gaining a comprehensive understanding of the key concepts and technologies related to information systems.

We are grateful to all those persons as well as various books, manuals, periodicals, magazines, journals etc. that helped in the preparation of this book. In spite of the best efforts, it is possible that some errors may have occurred into the compilation and editing of the book. Further queries, constructive suggestions and criticisms for the improvement of the book are always welcomed and shall be thankfully acknowledged.

Vinay Chandra

Samir Sinh

Contents

Section 1

Background

Chapter 1

Introductory Chapter: Information Systems

1. Introduction

Information systems (IS) are abundant and crucial for the functioning of society and day-to-day living. IS are often misunderstood and confused with databases, serving as simply a repository for data. It is important to realize that IS embody the following:

- Hardware/networks
- Software
- Data
- Procedures
- People

IS may be used in different ways, but a fundamental role is to take data and turn it into information, and then transform the information into organizational knowledge [1].

IS are used for a variety of different applications, ranging from business operations and management information through to decision support [2]. They have evolved from the initial static database systems to highly distributed cloud-based systems that incorporate AI, machine learning, and edge computing. Many organizations use information systems to manage resources, improve efficiency, and compete in global markets. Public services (e.g., healthcare, transport) rely on information systems for day-to-day operation as well as the management of resources and capacity planning.

It is important to realize the role that people play in IS [3]. People are often overlooked in areas of computing and IT, but their inclusion in all aspects of the IS cycle is crucial. People are involved in IS at different levels, namely the following:

- Identifying the need for IS
- Developing IS
- Supporting IS
- Using IS

The systems analyst and the team of developers play a crucial role in the design and development of IS. Equally, database administrators, information officers, support analysts, and security specialists are essential to keep IS operational. Finally, it is important to not lose sight of the users of IS, which is an issue reflected in the book.

References

[1] Irani Z, Sharif AM, Love PE. Linking knowledge transformation to information systems evaluation. European Journal of Information Systems. 2005;**14**(3):213-228

[2] Al-Mamary YH, Shamsuddin A, Aziati N. The role of different types of information systems in business organizations: A review. International Journal of Research. 2014;**1**(7):333-339

[3] Dumas M, Van der Aalst WM, Ter Hofstede AH. Process-Aware Information Systems: Bridging People and Software Through Process Technology. New Jersey, US: John Wiley & Sons; 2005. DOI: 10.1002/0471741442. ISBN: 9780471741442

Chapter 2

Basic Concepts of Information Systems

Abstract

This chapter covers the basic concepts of the information systems (IS) field to prepare the reader to quickly approach the book's other chapters: the Definition of information, the notion of system, and, more particularly, information systems. We also discuss the typology of IS according to the managerial level and decision-making in the IS. Furthermore, we describe information systems applications covering functional areas and focusing on the execution of business processes across the enterprise, including all management levels. We briefly discuss the aspects related to IS security that ensure the protection and integrity of information. We continue our exploration by presenting several metrics, mainly financial, to assess the added value of IS in companies. Next, we present a brief description of a very fashionable approach to make the information system evolve in all coherence, which is the urbanization of IS. We conclude this chapter with some IS challenges focusing on the leading causes of IS implementation's failure and success.

Keywords: information, system, information system, IS typology, Decision-making, IS applications, IS security, IS evaluation, IS evolution, and IS challenges

1. Introduction

According to Russell Ackoff [1], a systems theorist and professor of organizational change, the content of the human mind can be classified into three categories:

1. **Data** represents a fact or an event statement unrelated to other things. Data is generally used regarding hard facts. This can be a mathematical symbol or text used to identify, describe, or represent something like temperature or a person. The data simply exists and has no meaning beyond its existence (in itself). It can exist in any form, usable or not. The data exists in different formats, such as text, image, sound, or even video.

2. **Information** is data combined with meaning. Information embodies the understanding of a relationship as the relationship between cause and effect [2]. Ex: The temperature dropped 15 degrees, then it started to rain. A temperature reading of 100 can have different meanings when combined with the term Fahrenheit or with the term Celsius. More semantics can be added if more context for the temperature read is added, such as the fact that this temperature concerns a liquid or a gas or the seasonal norm of 20°. In other words, information is data that has meaning through relational connection. According to Ackoff, information is useful data; it provides answers to the questions: "who," "what," "where," and "when."

3. **Knowledge** can be seen as information combined with experience, context, and interpretation. Knowledge constitutes an additional semantic level derived from information via a process. Sometimes this process is observational. Ackoff defines it as applying data and information; knowledge provides answers to the question "how" For example, what happens in cold weather for aircraft managers? Observational knowledge engineers interpret cold by its impact, which is the ice that can form on an aircraft by reducing aerodynamic thrust and potentially hampering the performance of its control surfaces [2].

IF temperature < = 0° C THEN cold = true;
Cold IF == right THEN notify personnel to remove ice from aircraft.

Indeed, knowledge is the appropriate collection of information such that it intends to be useful. Knowledge is a deterministic process. Memorization of information leads to knowledge. Knowledge represents a pattern and provides a high level of predictability regarding what is being described or will happen next.

Ex: If the humidity is very high and the temperature drops drastically, the atmosphere is unlikely to hold the humidity so that it rains.

This knowledge has a useful meaning, but its integration in a context will infer new knowledge. For example, a student memorizes or accumulates knowledge of the multiplication Table. A student can answer 2 × 2 because this knowledge is in the multiplication table. Nevertheless, when asked for 1267 × 300, he cannot answer correctly because he cannot dip into the multiplication table. To answer such a question correctly requires a real cognitive and analytical capacity that exists in the next level ... comprehension. In computer jargon, most of the applications we use (modeling, simulation, etc.) use stored knowledge.

2. System definition

The system is an aggregated "whole" where each component interacts with at least one other component of the system. The components or parts of a system can be real or abstract.

All system components work toward a standard system goal. A system can contain several subsystems. It can be connected to other systems.

A system is a collection of elements or components that interact to achieve goals. The elements themselves and the relationships between them determine how the system works. Systems have inputs, processing mechanisms, outputs, and feedback mechanisms. A system processes the input to create the output [3].

- Input is the activity of collecting and capturing data.

- Processing involves the transformation of inputs into outputs such as computation, for example.

- Output is about producing useful information, usually in the form of documents and reports. The output of one system can become the input of another system. For example, the output of a system, which processes sales orders, can be used as input to a customer's billing system. Computers typically produce output to printers and display to screens. The output can also be reports and documents written by hand or produced manually.

- Finally, feedback or feedback is information from the system used to modify inputs or treatments as needed.

3. Information system definition

An information system (IS) is a set of interrelated components that collect, manipulate, store and disseminate information and provide a feedback mechanism to achieve a goal. The feedback mechanism helps organizations achieve their goals by increasing profits, improving customer service [3], and supporting decision-making and control in organizations [4].

Companies use information systems to increase revenues and reduce costs.

In organizations, information systems are structured around four essential elements, proposed in the 1960s by Harold Leavitt (**Figure 1**). The pattern is known as the "Leavitt Diamond."

1. **Technology**: The IT (Information Technology) of an IS includes the hardware, software, and telecommunications equipment used to capture, process, store and disseminate information. Today, most IS are IT-based because modern IT enables efficient operations execution and effective management in all sizes.

2. **Task**: activities necessary for the production of a good or service. These activities are supported by the flow of material, information, and knowledge between the different participants.

3. **Person**: The people component of an information system encompasses all the people directly involved in the system. These people include the managers who define the goals of the system, the users, and the developers.

4. **Structure**: The organizational structure and information systems component refers to the relationship between individuals people components. Thus, it encompasses hierarchical structures, relationships, and systems for evaluating people.

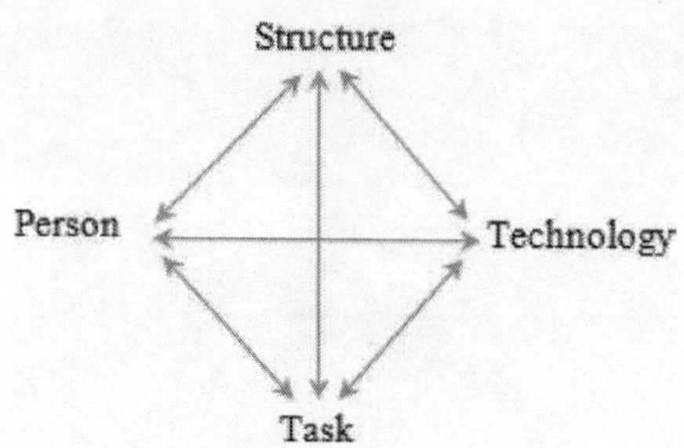

Figure 1.
Leavitt's diamond: A socio-technical view of IS.

4. Typology of information systems

A company has systems to support the different managerial levels. These systems include transaction processing systems, management information systems, decision support systems, and dedicated business intelligence systems.

Companies use information systems so that accurate and up-to-date information is available when needed [5].

Within the same organization, executives at different hierarchy levels have very different information requirements, and different types of information systems have evolved to meet their needs. A common approach for examining the types of information systems used within organizations is to classify them according to their roles at different organizational structure levels, and this approach is called a vertical approach. Indeed, the organization is considered a management pyramid at four levels (**Figure 2**):

- **On the lowest level**, staff perform routine day-to-day operations such as selling goods and issuing payment receipts.
- **Operational management** in which managers are responsible for overseeing transaction control and deal with issues that may arise.
- **Tactical management,** which has the prerogative of making decisions on budgets, setting objectives, identifying trends, and planning short-term business activities.
- **Strategic management** is responsible for defining its long-term objectives and positioning concerning its competitors or its industry.

4.1 Transaction processing system (TPS)

At the operational level, managers need systems that keep track of the organization for necessary activities and operations, such as sales and material flow in a factory. A transaction processing system is a computer system that performs and records the routine (daily) operations necessary for managing affairs, such as keeping employee records, payroll, shipping merchandise, keeping records, accounting and treasury.

At this level, the primary purpose of systems is to answer routine questions and monitor transactions flow through the organization.

At the operational level, tasks, resources, and objectives are predefined and highly structured. The decision to grant credit to a customer, for example, is made

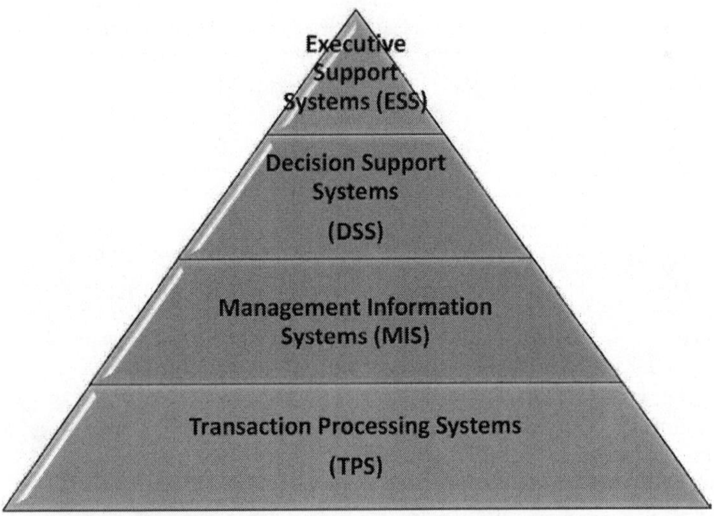

Figure 2.
Information Systems types according to managerial level.

by a primary supervisor according to predefined criteria. All that needs to be determined is whether the client meets the criteria.

4.2 Management information systems (MIS)

Middle managers need systems to help with oversight, control, decision making, and administrative activities. The main question that this type of system must answer is: is everything working correctly?

Its role is to summarize and report on essential business operations using data provided by transaction processing systems. Primary transaction data is synthesized and aggregated, and it is usually presented in reports produced regularly.

4.3 Decision support systems (DSS)

DSS supports decision-making for unusual and rapidly evolving issues, for which there are no fully predefined procedures. This type of system attempts to answer questions such as: What would impact production schedules if we were to double sales for December? What would the level of Return on investment be if the plant schedule were delayed by more than six months?

While DSSs use internal information from TPS and MIS systems, they also leverage external sources, such as stock quotes or competitor product prices. These systems use a variety of models to analyze the data. The system can answer questions such as: Considering customer's delivery schedule and the freight rate offered, which vessel should be assigned, and what fill rate to maximize profits? What is the optimum speed at which a vessel can maximize profit while meeting its delivery schedule?

4.4 Executive support system (ESS)

ESS helps top management make decisions. They address exceptional decisions requiring judgment, assessment, and a holistic view of the business situation because there is no procedure to be followed to resolve a given issue at this level.

ESS uses graphics and data from many sources through an interface that senior managers easily understand. ESS is designed to integrate data from the external environment, such as new taxes or competitor data, and integrate aggregate data from MIS and DSS. ESSs filter, synthesize and track critical data. Particular attention is given to displaying this data because it contributes to the rapid assimilation of these top management figures. Increasingly, these systems include business intelligence analysis tools to identify key trends and forecasts.

5. Decision making and information systems

Decision-making in companies is often associated with top management. Today, employees at the operational level are also responsible for individual decisions since information systems make information available at all company levels.

So decisions are made at all levels of the company.

Although some of these decisions are common, routine, and frequent, the value of improving any single decision may be small, but improving hundreds or even thousands of "small" decisions can add value to the business.

Not all situations that require decisions are the same. While some decisions result in actions that significantly impact the organization and its future, others are much less important and play a relatively minor role. A decision's impact is a criterion that can differentiate between decision situations and the degree of the decision's structuring. Many situations are very structured, with well-defined entrances and exits. For example, it is relatively easy to determine the amount of an employee's pay if we have the appropriate input data (for example, the number of hours worked and their hourly wage rate), and all the rules of relevant decision (for example, if the hours worked during a week are more than 40, then the overtime must be calculated), and so on. In this type of situation, it is relatively easy to develop information systems that can be used to help (or even automate) the decision.

In contrast, some decision situations are very complex and unstructured, where no specific decision rules can be easily identified. As an example, consider the following task: "Design a new vehicle that is a convertible (with a retractable hardtop), has a high safety rating, and is esthetically pleasing to a reasonably broad audience. No predefined solution to this task finalizing a design will involve many compromises and require considerable knowledge and expertise.

Examples of Types of decisions, according to managerial level, are presented in **Table 1**.

Generally speaking, structured decisions are more common at lower levels of the organization, while unstructured problems are more common at higher business levels.

The more structured the decision, the easier it is to automate. If it is possible to derive an algorithm that can be used to make an efficient decision and the input data to the algorithm can be obtained at a reasonable cost, it generally makes sense to automate the decision.

Davenport and Harris [6] proposed a framework for the categorization of applications used for decision automation. Most of the systems they describe include some expert systems, often combined with DSS and/or EIS aspects. The categories they provided include Solution Configuration, Optimization of Performance, Routing or Segmentation of Decisions, Business Regulatory Compliance, Fraud Detection, Dynamic Forecasting, and Operational Control.

Many business decision situations are not very structured, and therefore cannot (or should not) be fully automated.

5.1 A particular type of decision support system: geographic information systems

Data visualization tools allow users to see patterns and relationships in large amounts of data that would be difficult to discern if the data had been presented in tabular form, for example.

Geographic Information Systems (GIS) helps decision-makers visualize issues requiring knowledge about people's geographic distribution or other resources. GIS software links the location data of points, lines, and areas on a map. Some GIS have modeling capabilities to modify data and simulate the impact of these modifications. For example, GIS could help the government calculate response times to natural disasters and other emergencies or help banks identify the best replacement for installing new branches or ATMs of tickets.

Geographic (or geospatial) information refers not only to things that exist (or are being planned) on specific locations on the Earth's surface but also to events such as traffic congestion, flooding, and other events such as an open-air festival [7].

Its scope and granularity characterize this information:

- Location, extent, and coverage are essential aspects of geographic information.

- Granularity, for example, geometric information, can be concise or fuzzy depending on the application.

Decision level	Characteristics of decisions	Examples of decisions
Top Management	Unstructured	Decide whether or not to come into the market
		Approve the budget allocated to capital
		Decide on long-term goals
Intermediate management	Semi-structured	Design a marketing plan
		Develop a departmental budget
		Design a website for the company
Operational management	Structured	Determine the overtime hours
		Determine the rules for stock replenishment
		Grant credit to customers
		Offer special offers to customers

Table 1.
Types of decisions according to managerial level.

GIS is used to capture, store, analyze, and visualize data that describes part of the Earth's surface, technical and administrative entities, and the results of geosciences, economics, and ecological applications.

- It is a computer system with a database observing the spatial distribution of objects, activities, or events described by points, lines, or surfaces.
- It is a comprehensive collection of tools for capturing, storing, extracting, transforming, and visualizing real-world spatial data for applications.
- It is an information system containing all the data of the territory, the atmosphere, the surface of the Earth, and the lithosphere, allowing the systematic capture, the update, the manipulation, and the analysis of these data standardized reference framework.
- It is a decision support system that integrates spatial data into a problem-solving environment.

Other definitions of GIS exist depending on the point of view of application [7], a GIS can be considered as

- A collection of spatial data with storage and retrieval functions
- A collection of algorithmic and functional tools
- A set of hardware and software components necessary for processing geospatial data
- A particular type of information technology
- A gold mine for answers to geospatial questions
- A model of spatial relations and spatial recognition.

Typically, a GIS provides functions for the storage and retrieval, interrogation and visualization, transformation, geometric and thematic analysis of information.

Indeed, geographic/geospatial information is ubiquitous, as seen on mobile devices such as cell phones, maps, satellite images, positioning and routing services, and even 3D simulations, gaining popularity from increasingly essential segments of the consumers.

Technological advances in recent years have transformed classical GIS into new forms of geospatial analysis tools, namely:

- Web-based and service-oriented approaches have led to a client–server architecture.

- Mobile technology has made GIS ubiquitous in smartphones, tablets, and laptops (opening up new markets).

6. Information systems applications

IS applications cover functional areas and focus on the execution of business processes across the enterprise, including all management levels.

There are several categories of business applications: Enterprise Resource Planning (ERP), Supply Chain Management systems (SCM), Customer Relationship Management systems (CRM), electronic commerce or e-commerce, Knowledge Management systems or KM, and Business Intelligence or BI. The categories of business applications dealt with in this section cover all managerial levels since KMS are mainly intended for top management (ESS), SCMs, CRMs, and BI for mid-level management (MIS and DSS), ERP and e-commerce dedicated to the transactional level (TPS or basic or operational).

However, it is useful to specify that some ERP systems, such as the global giant SAP, offer versions of its software package covering these different categories, including SCM and CRM.

6.1 ERP, Enterprise resource planning

ERPs allow business processes related to production, finance and accounting, sales and marketing, and human resources to be integrated into a single software system. Information that was previously fragmented across many different systems is integrated into a single system with a single, comprehensive database that multiple business stakeholders can use.

An ERP system centralizes an organization's data, and the processes it applies are the processes that the organization must adopt [8]. When an ERP provider designs a module, it must implement the rules of the associated business processes. ERP systems apply best management practices. In other words, when an organization implements ERP, it also improves its management as part of ERP integration. For many organizations, implementing an ERP system is an excellent opportunity to improve their business practices and upgrade their software simultaneously. Nevertheless, integrating an ERP represents a real challenge: Are the processes integrated into the ERP better than those currently used? Furthermore, if the integration is booming, and the organization operates the same as its competitors, how do you differentiate yourself?

ERPs are configurable according to the specificities of each organization. For organizations that want to continue using their processes or even design new ones, ERP systems provide means for customizing these processes. However, the burden of maintenance falls on the organizations themselves in the case of ERP customization.

Organizations will need to consider the following decision carefully: should they accept the best practice processes embedded in the ERP system or develop their processes? If the choice is ERP, process customization should only concern processes essential to its competitive advantage.

6.2 E-commerce, electronic commerce

Electronic commerce is playing an increasingly important role in organizations with their customers.

E-commerce enables market expansion with minimal capital investment, improves the supply and marketing of products and services. Nevertheless, there is still a need for universally accepted standards to ensure the quality and security of information and sufficient telecommunications bandwidth.

The three main categories of e-commerce are Business-to-Consumer (B2C), Business-to-Business (B2B), and Consumer-to-Consumer (C2C).

- Business-to-Consumer (B2C) e-commerce involves the retailing of products and services to individual customers. Amazon, which sells books, software, and music to individual consumers, is an example of B2C e-commerce.

- Business-to-Business (B2B), e-commerce involves the sale of goods and services between businesses. The ChemConnect website for buying and selling chemicals and plastics is an example of B2B e-commerce.

- Consumer-to-Consumer (C2C), this type of e-commerce involves consumers selling directly to consumers. For example, eBay, the giant web-based auction site, allows individuals to sell their products to other consumers by auctioning their goods, either to the highest bidder or through a fixed price.

6.3 SCM, Information systems for supply chain management

Information systems for the management of the supply chain or SCM make it possible to manage its suppliers' relations. These systems help suppliers and distributors share information about orders, production, inventory levels, and delivery of products and services so that they can source, produce and deliver goods and services efficiently.

The ultimate goal is to get the right amount of products from their suppliers at a lower cost and time. Additionally, these systems improve profitability by enabling managers to optimize scheduling decisions for procurement, production, and distribution.

Anomalies in the supply chain, such as parts shortages, underutilized storage areas, prolonged storage of finished products, or high transportation cost, are caused by inaccurate or premature information. For example, manufacturers may stock an excessive amount of parts because they do not know precisely the dates of upcoming deliveries from suppliers. Alternatively, conversely, the manufacturer may order a small number of raw materials because they do not have precise information about their needs. These supply chain inefficiencies squander up to 25 percent of the company's operating costs.

If a manufacturer has precise information on the exact number of units of the product demanded by customers, on what date, and its exact production rate, it would be possible to implement a successful strategy called "just in time" (just-in-time strategy). Raw materials would be received precisely when production needed them, and finished products would be shipped off the assembly line with no need for storage.

However, there are always uncertainties in a supply chain because many events cannot be predicted, such as late deliveries from suppliers, defective parts or non-conforming raw materials, or even breakdowns in the production process. To cope with these kinds of contingencies and keep their customers happy, manufacturers often deal with these uncertainties by stocking more materials or products than they need. The safety stock acts as a buffer against probable supply chain anomalies. While managing excess inventory is expensive, a low stock fill rate is also costly because orders can be canceled.

6.4 CRM, Information systems for customer relationship management

CRM aims to manage customer relationships by coordinating all business processes that deal with customers' sales and marketing. The goal is to optimize revenue, customer satisfaction, and customer loyalty. This collected information helps companies identify, attract and retain the most profitable customers, and provide better service to existing customers and increase sales.

The CRM captures and integrates the data of the company's customers. It consolidates data, analyzes it, and distributes the results to different systems and customer touchpoints throughout the company. A point of contact (touchpoint, contact point) is a means of interaction with the customer, such as telephone, e-mail, customer service, conventional mail, website, or even a sales store, by retail.

Well-designed CRM systems provide a single view of the company's customers, which is useful for improving sales and customer service quality. Such systems also provide customers with a single view of the business regardless of their contact point or usage.

CRM systems provide data and analytical tools to answer these types of questions: "What is the value of a customer to the business" "Who are the most loyal customers?" "Who are the most profitable customers" and "What products are profitable customers buying?"

Businesses use the answers to these questions to acquire new customers, improve service quality, support existing customers, tailor offerings to customer preferences, and deliver escalating services to retain profitable customers.

6.5 KM, knowledge management

Some companies perform better than others because they know how to create, produce, and deliver products and services. This business knowledge is difficult to emulate, is unique, and can be leveraged and deliver long-term strategic benefits. Knowledge Management Systems or KMS enable organizations to manage processes better to collect and apply knowledge and expertise. These systems collect all the relevant knowledge and experiences in the company and make them available to everyone to improve business processes and decision management.

Knowledge management systems can take many different forms, but the primary goals are: 1) facilitating communication between knowledge workers within an organization, and 2) to make explicit the expertise of a few and make it available to many.

Consider an international consulting firm, for example. The company employs thousands of consultants across many countries. The consultancy team in Spain may be trying to resolve a client's problem, very similar to a consultancy team in Singapore that has already been solved. Rather than reinventing the solution, it would be much more useful for the Spain team to use the Singapore team's knowledge.

One way to remedy this situation is to store case histories from which employees worldwide can access (via the Internet) and search for cases (using a search engine) according to their respective needs. If the case documentation is of good quality (accurate, timely, complete), the consultants will share and benefit from each other's experiences, and the knowledge gained.

Unfortunately, it is often difficult to get employees to contribute meaningfully to the knowledge base (as they are probably more concerned with moving forward on their next engagements with customers rather than documenting their past experiences). For such systems to have any chance of success, the work organization must change, such as establishing a reward system for cases captured and well documented.

6.6 BI, business intelligence

The term Business Intelligence (BI) is generally used to describe a type of information system designed to help decision-makers learn about trends and identify relationships in large volumes of data. Typically, BI software is used in conjunction with large databases or data warehouses. While the specific capabilities of BI systems vary, most can be used for specialized reporting (e.g., aggregated data relating to multiple dimensions), ad-hoc queries, and trend analysis.

As with knowledge management systems, the value of business intelligence systems can be hampered in several ways. The quality of the data that is captured and stored is not guaranteed. Besides, the database (or data warehouse) may lack essential data (for example, ice cream sales are likely to correlate with temperature; without the temperature information, it may be difficult to identify why it is. There has been an increase or decrease in sales of ice cream). A third challenge is the lack of mastery of data analysts over the context of the organization's operations, even if they are proficient in BI software. In contrast, a manager has mastery of the organization but does not know how to use BI software. As a result, it is common to have a team (a manager associated with a data analyst) to get the most information (and/or knowledge) from a business intelligence system.

7. Information systems security

Unlike physical assets, the information does not necessarily disappear when it has been stolen. If an organization holds confidential information such as a new manufacturing process, it may be uploaded by an unauthorized person and remain available to the organization.

Exposing information to unauthorized personnel constitutes a breach of confidentiality.

Another type of system failure happens when the integrity of information is no longer guaranteed. In other words, rather than unauthorized exposure of information, there are unauthorized changes of information. A corporate website containing documentation on how to configure or repair its products could suffer severe financial harm if an intruder could change instructions, leading to customers misconfigure or even ruin the purchased product.

Finally, the denial of access to information or the unavailability of information represents another type of information failure. For example, if a doctor is prevented from accessing a patient's test results, the patient may suffer needlessly or even die. A commercial website could lose significant sales if its website were down for an extended period.

Understanding the potential causes of system failure enables appropriate action to be taken to avoid them. There are a wide variety of potential threats to an organization's information systems.

Human threats are the most complicated to manage because they include a wide variety of behaviors. To illustrate how the level of detail can vary, some relevant subcategories include:

- Accidental behavior by members of the organization, technical support staff, and customers of the organization
- Malicious behavior by someone inside or outside the organization
- Other categories of threats include:
- A natural event: flood, fire, tornado, ice storm, earthquake, pandemic flu
- Environmental elements: chemical spill, gas line explosion.
- Technical Threat: Hardware or software failure
- Operational Threat: a faulty process that unintentionally compromises the confidentiality, integrity, or availability of information. For example, an operational procedure that allows application programmers to upgrade software without test or notification system operators can result in prolonged outages.

It is possible to categorize the various checks intended to avoid a failure, such as:

1. Management controls management processes that identify system requirements such as confidentiality, integrity, and availability of information and provide for various management controls to ensure that these requirements are met.

2. Operational controls: include the day-to-day processes associated with the provision of information services.

3. Technical controls: concern the technical capacities integrated into the IT infrastructure to support the increased confidentiality, integrity, and availability of information services.

A widely cited Gartner research report concludes that "people directly cause 80% of downtime in critical application services. The remaining 20% are caused by technological failures, environmental failure or a natural disaster".

Often, these failures are the result of software modifications such as adding new features or misconfiguring servers or network devices.

IT professionals should ensure that system changes are prioritized and tested and that all interested parties are notified of proposed changes.

8. Information systems assessment

Perceptible benefits can be quantified and assigned a monetary value. Imperceptible benefits, such as more efficient customer service or improved decision making, cannot be immediately quantified but can lead to quantifiable long-term gain [4].

System performance can be measured in different ways.

8.1 Efficiency

Efficiency is often referred to as "doing the things right" or doing things right. Efficiency can be defined as the ratio of output to input. In other words, a company is more efficient if it produces more with the same amount of resources or if it produces the same amount of output with a lower investment of resources, or - even better - produces more with less input. In other words, the company achieves improvements in terms of efficiency by reducing the waste of resources while maximizing Productivity.

Each time an item is sold or ordered, the manager updates the quantity of the item sold in the inventory system. The manager needs to check the sales to determine which items have been sold the most and restocked. This considerably reduces the manager's time to manage his stock (limit input to achieve the same output). So efficiency is a measure of what is produced divided by what is consumed [3].

8.2 Effectiveness

Effectiveness is measured based on the degree achieved in achieving system objectives. It can be calculated by dividing the objectives achieved by the total of the objectives set.

Effectiveness is denoted as "doing the right thing" or doing the things necessary or right. It is possible to define effectiveness as an organization's ability to achieve its stated goals and objectives. Typically, a business more significant is the one that makes the best decisions and can carry them out.

For example, to better meet its various customers' needs, an organization may create or improve its products and services founded on data collected from them and information accumulated from sales activities. In other words, information systems help organizations better understand their customers and deliver the products and services that customers desire. Collecting customer data on an individual basis will help the organization provide them with personalized service.

The manager can also ask customers what kind of products and services customers would like to buy in the future, trying to anticipate their needs. With the information gathered, the manager will order the customers' products and stop ordering unpopular products.

In what follows, we present several formulas established to measure efficiency and effectiveness resulting from the information systems use. Indeed, the impact of an information system on an organization can be assessed using financial measures.

8.3 Financial measures of managerial performance

When the information system is implemented, management will certainly want to assess whether the system has succeeded in achieving its objectives. Often this assessment is challenging to achieve. The business can use financial metrics such as Productivity, Return On Investment (ROI), net present value, and other performance metrics explained in the following:

8.3.1 Return on investment

Return on investment, denoted as a Return rate, is a financial ratio that measures the amount gained or lost compared to the amount initially invested.

An information system with a positive return on investment indicates that this system can improve its efficiency.

The advantage of using Return on investment is that it is possible to quantify the costs and benefits of introducing an information system. Therefore, it is possible to use this metric to compare different systems and see which systems can help the organization be more efficient and/or more effective.

8.3.2 Productivity

Developing information systems that measure Productivity and control is a crucial element for most organizations. Productivity is a measure of produced output divided by required input. A higher production level for a given entry-level means greater Productivity; a lower output level for a given entry-level means lower Productivity. Values assigned to productivity levels are not always based on hours worked. Productivity may be based on the number of raw materials used, the quality obtained, or the time to produce the goods or services. According to other parameters and with other organizations in the same industry, Productivity's value has to mean only compared to other Productivity periods.

8.3.3 Profit growth

Another measure of the SI value is the increase in profit or the growth in realized profits. For example, a mail-order company installs an order processing system that generates 7 percent growth in profits over the previous year.

8.3.4 Market share

Market share is the percentage of sales of a product or service relative to the overall market. If installing a new online catalog increases sales, it could help increase the company's market share by, for example, 20 percent.

8.3.5 Customer satisfaction

Although customer satisfaction is difficult to quantify, many companies measure their information systems performance based on internal and external feedback. Some companies use surveys and questionnaires to determine whether investments have resulted in increased customer satisfaction.

8.3.6 Total cost of ownership

Another way to measure the value of information systems has been developed by the Gartner Group and is called the Total Cost of Ownership (TCO). This approach allocates the total costs between acquiring the technology, technical support, and administrative costs. Other costs are added to the TCO, namely: retooling and training costs. TCO can help develop a more accurate estimate of total costs for systems ranging from small computers to large mainframe systems.

9. Information systems evolution

The evolution of information technologies leads to the reflection on new approaches that set up more flexible, more scalable architectures to meet its agility needs. The urbanization of information systems is one such approach.

9.1 Definition of the urbanization of information systems

The company's information system's urbanization is an IT discipline consisting of developing its information system to guarantee its consistency with its objectives and business. By taking into account its external and internal constraints while taking advantage of the opportunities of the IT state of the art.

This discipline is based on a series of concepts modeled on those of the urbanization of human habitat (organization of cities, territory), concepts that have been reused in IT to formalize or model the information system.

Town planning defines rules and a coherent, stable, and modular framework, to which the various stakeholders refer for any investment decision relating to the management of the information system.

In other words, to urbanize is to lead the information systems' continuous transformation to simplify it and ensure its consistency.

The challenges of urbanization consist of managing complexity, communicating and federating work, considering organizational constraints, and guiding technological choices.

9.2 Stages of urbanization

9.2.1 Definition of objectives

Define and frame the objectives of the project, define the scope, develop the schedule.

9.2.2 Analysis of the existing situation

Carry out the inventory, organize the work, and present the deliverables. More precisely, list the assets and map the different layers (business, functional, application, and technical):

- Business Architecture

  Identify "business processes": Who does what and why? The description of the processes is done with BPMN, EPC formalisms, etc. This step is tricky and may require the use of exploration methods. However, it does improve the overall understanding and increase the possibilities for optimization

- Functional architecture

  Identify the "functional block": What do we need to carry out the business processes? Here, we are based on a classic division into zones (exchanges, core business, reference data, production data, support activities, management). This step's difficulty lies in choosing the right level of detail and remaining consistent with business processes. However, it provides a hierarchical presentation and makes it easier to break down the work.

- Application Architecture

  Identify the applications: How to achieve the functionalities? This step is based on a classic N-Tiers division. However, it is not easy to provide value and solutions compared to functional architecture. This stage lays the foundations for the realization (major technological choices, etc.).

- System Architecture

  Identify the technical components: With what and where the applications work, it is based on a classic division into technical areas (security, storage, etc.). It is not easy to make the connection between applications and servers. This step brings concrete and structuring and is essential to assess the cost of the system.

9.2.3 Identification of the target IS

Impact on the different layers, consideration of constraints (human, material, etc.), design of costed scenarios, and arbitration of the choice of a target.

9.2.4 Development of the trajectory

How to organize the work, frame and then refine the budgets, design and plan projects, define the support strategy, set up an organization, contributions, roles, and responsibilities of actors.

At the end of this process, a Land Use Plan (LUP) is defined. It is a report consisting of:

- Summaries of the orientations chosen as well as the justifications for the options selected.
- A definition of areas, neighborhoods, and blocks.
- Existing and target maps (process, functional, application, and technical mapping).
- Additional documents (interview reports, list of people and organizational entities, etc.)

The goal is to identify the gaps between the existing and the principles of urbanization and establish changes by describing the actions and their corresponding cost.

In practice, the urbanization process is very cumbersome to implement. On the one hand, it requires the participation of many actors in the organization, and on the other hand, the analysis is very long. As a result, needs to change, and LUP is no longer necessarily suitable.

10. Information systems challenges

The reasons for a successful or unsuccessful IS implementation are complex and contested by different stakeholders and from the various perspectives involved. Developers tend to focus on the system's technical validity in terms of execution, operation, and evolution. Other qualities are often considered, such as security, maintainability, scalability, stability, and availability. All of these criteria are considered to be signs of successful IS Development.

The failure of an IS can be defined as: either the system put in place does not meet the user's expectations or does not function properly. The reasons for failure are as divergent as the projects.

The perspective of project management, on the other hand, tends to focus on the consumption of resources. The project delivered with the initial budget and within the allotted time is considered a successful project. Nelson [9] analyzed 99 SI projects and identified 36 classic errors. He categorized these errors into four categories: process, people, product, and technology. The last category concerns the factors leading to IS failures based on the misuse of modern technologies.

The seminal article by DeLone and McLean [10] suggested that IS success should be the preeminent dependent variable for the IS domain. These researchers proposed a taxonomy of six interdependent variables to define the IS' success as the system's quality, the quality of information, the IS, user satisfaction, individual impact, and organizational impact.

One of the significant extensions to this proposition is the dimension of the IT department's quality of service [11].

Either way, the use of the system is seen as a sign of its success. The IS use level is incorporated into most IS success models [11, 12]. These models show the complexity of measuring user satisfaction because, even in the same organization, some user groups may be more or less enthusiastic than others to use the new information system.

In the current global context of the covid pandemic, it appears clear that information systems that integrate web and mobile technologies can positively contribute to the monitoring of contaminated cases and therefore minimize the risks of contamination provided that users adhere to this movement for the benefit of all [13]. A truly global, rapid, and efficient decision-making process is enabled by the integration of information systems from distributed sources [14].

11. Conclusion

To conclude this introductive chapter, we present its key ideas:

- Levels of information are data, information, and knowledge.
- The system is an aggregated "whole" where each component interacts with at least one other system component to achieve a goal.
- An information system can be defined as a set of interconnected components that gather, process, store and dispense information to support decision making and control in an organization. An IS can be seen as a socio-technical system. The technical part includes the technology and the processes, while the social part includes the people and the structure.
- The role of information systems is to solve an organization's problems concerning its information needs
- A company has systems to support the different managerial levels: transaction processing systems, management information systems, decision support systems, and systems dedicated to business intelligence.
- Decisions can be operational or strategic.
- There are several categories of business applications: enterprise resource planning, supply chain management systems, customer relationship management systems, knowledge management systems, and business intelligence.

- Among the failures that can affect IS a violation of confidentiality, integrity, and availability of information.
- The controls intended to avoid the IS's security failures include management controls, operational controls, and technical controls.
- The information system's performance can be measured according to efficiency, effectiveness, Return on investment, Productivity, customer satisfaction, etc.
- Urbanizing an information system means directing its continuous transformation to guarantee its consistency
- The reasons for a successful or unsuccessful implementation of an IS are complex and contested by the various stakeholders and from the various perspectives involved.

References

[1] Ackoff R L. From Data to Wisdom. Journal of Applied Systems Analysis; 1989, 16, 3-9.

[2] Watson R T. Information Systems. Global Text Project, University of Georgia, Collection open source textbooks; 2007, 1-33.

[3] Stair R M, Reynolds G. Fundamentals of business information systems. Thomson Learning; 2008, 118-129

[4] Laudon K C, Laudon J P. Management information systems: managing the digital firm. Edition 12, Prentice Hall; 2012.

[5] Van Belle J P, Nash J, Eccles M. Discovering Information Systems: an exploratory approach. University of Cape Town; 2010.

[6] Davenport T H, Harris J G. Automated Decision Making Comes of Age. Sloan Management Review; 2005, 46(4), 83-89.

[7] Kresse, W., & Danko, D. M. Springer handbook of geographic information. Springer Science & Business Media; 2012.

[8] Bourgeois, D. T. Information Systems for Business and Beyond. Washington: The Saylor Academy; 2014.

[9] Nelson, R. R. (2007). IT project management: infamous failures, classic mistakes, and best practices. MIS Quarterly Executive, 6 (2), 67-78.

[10] DeLone, W.H., and McLean, E.R. (1992) Information systems success: The quest for the dependent variable. Information Systems Research, 3 (1), 60-95.

[11] Petter, Stacie, William DeLone, and Ephraim R. McLean. (2013). Information systems success: The quest for the independent variables. Journal of Management Information Systems 29 (4), 7-62.

[12] Delone, William H., and Ephraim R. McLean, (2003). The DeLone and McLean model of information systems success: a ten-year update. Journal of management information systems 19 (4), 9-30.

[13] Ågerfalk, P. J., Conboy, K., & Myers, M. D. (2020). Information systems in the age of pandemics: COVID-19 and beyond.

[14] O'Leary, D. E. (2020). Evolving information systems and technology research issues for COVID-19 and other pandemics. Journal of Organizational Computing and Electronic Commerce, 30(1), 1-8.

Section 2

Applications

Chapter 3

Bayesian Networks for Decision Support in Emergency Response: A Model for Missing Person Investigations

Abstract

The successful operation of Emergency services (Police, Fire, Medical Emergency) relies heavily upon Information Systems and particularly Decision Support Systems. Missing person cases consume resources from the already overstretched resources of Police Forces. Such cases predominantly come from at-risk groups such as children in care, people suffering from depression, or elderly people suffering from dementia. This chapter reviews current practices used for missing person cases and describes a decision support model based on Bayesian networks.

Keywords: Bayesian networks, algorithms, missing persons, decision support, probability

1. Introduction

Emergency services face increasing demands in their challenges to keep the public safe and healthy. They typically utilize a variety of information systems to store data relating to previous incidents and recall data to assist with new incidents and tasks such as capacity planning. One particular class of information systems that play a vital role in emergency service operations is decision support systems. Such systems combine data and logic together with rules and heuristics to allow operational decisions to be made based on the domain knowledge embodied within the system. Typical examples of such systems are utilized by Police Forces in the development of search strategies for locating missing persons.

1.1 Missing persons

According to National Guidelines set out for UK Police Forces, A ***missing** person* is defined as:

'Anyone whose whereabouts cannot be established and where the circumstances are out of character or the context suggests the person may be subject of crime or at risk of harm to themselves or another'.

When someone is categorized as missing, the police will investigate their disappearance and try to find and safeguard them.

In 2013 the Guidelines introduced a second ***absent** person* category, defined as:

'A person not at a place where they are expected or required to be' and perceived to be 'not at any apparent risk'.

When someone is categorized as absent, no police response is required except to monitor and review the situation.

Typically absent cases involve individuals who go missing frequently (often referred to as frequent fliers). They are likely to be designated a missing person for the first few times that they are missing, but, if they return unharmed, thereafter they may be designated absent.

Missing person cases are both time consuming and resource intense, particularly in urban areas. **Figure 1** highlights the scale of misper cases facing UK Police Forces and the volume of calls generated from dealing with such cases.

Mispers come from a spectrum of the population. Many are children (teenagers) who go missing from care homes; others are adults with mental illness or depression. Cases also include elderly people suffering from dementia-related conditions. Murder (homicide) cases, manslaughter cases and death by misadventure often start out as misper cases until a body is located. Current practice relies on heuristics and localized domain knowledge. Social scientists will often interview mispers in the hope of eliciting knowledge in relation to mispers' intentions while they were missing. Typically, Police rely heavily on historical data and behavioral patterns. For example, many teenagers who go missing are found in local parks, where teenagers are known to congregate. Elderly people suffering from dementia may travel to a location associated with their past.

1.2 *Bayesian networks*

Many problems in machine learning are solved by using supervised learning techniques, in which specific training input patterns are input to the model. Supervised learning is often the preferred solution of choice and powerful models such as Neural Networks and Support Vector Machines (SVMs) are available to implement supervised learning solutions. However, many cases exist where supervised learning is not applicable, typically when there is not one target variable of interest but many, or when different variables might be available or missing for each data point. Such examples include diagnosis in medicine, with many different types of diseases, symptoms, and context information available for a given patient. In a similar fashion, the problem of predicting the location of a missing person, or the distance that they may have traveled, poses similar problems to those found in medicine.

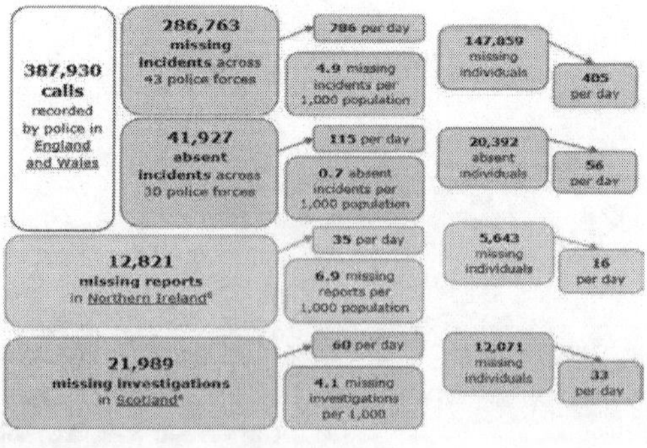

Figure 1.
Key statistics for missing person in the UK, 2016–2017.

Bayesian networks (BNs) can deal with such challenges. BNs are seen as a popular choice for probabilistic reasoning and machine learning problems that are difficult to address with supervised learning techniques. BNs are undergoing a renaissance amongst the machine learning community as an effective probabilistic model that can be used to assist decision support. Implemented as a graphical network and supported by libraries in Python and R (e.g. bnlearn and Pomegranate), they allow probability inferences to generate 'what if'? and 'which is best'? In addition to medicine, BNs have been successfully applied to genetics, search and rescue (SAR) and general classification problems.

The particular strengths and weaknesses of BN may be summarized as:

- They provide a natural way to handle missing data
- Suitable for small and incomplete datasets
- Combine different sources of knowledge
- Explicit treatment of uncertainty and support for decision analysis
- Fast response to queries

The main drawback of BNs is their inability to deal with continuous data, which needs to be discretized. Section 3 describes the application of BNs to develop a model to assist the decision-making process for misper cases. A more detailed consideration of the approach is described in [1].

2. Current approaches for missing person searches

The sections below review the main research approaches for dealing with missing person cases, which range from empirical techniques to formalized approaches.

2.1 Bayesian networks for search and rescue

There is some notable research concerned with the use of BN for Search And Rescue (SAR), in relation to people and objects who have either become lost or gone missing by accident. The distinction of course is that at-risk misper groups have intentionally gone missing, whilst SAR cases deal with entities, which have unintentionally become lost. The most notable use of Bayesian inference for search techniques was that of the search for Air France Flight AF 447, which crashed into the Atlantic on 1st June 2009 [2]. After 2 years of unsuccessful searching, the team used a Bayesian procedure developed for search planning to produce the posterior target location distribution. The distribution was used to guide the search and the wreckage was located within a week.

Reference [3] describes a Bayesian approach to modeling lost person behaviors based on terrain features in Wilderness Search and Rescue. The approach uses a first-order Markov transition matrix for generating a temporal, posterior predictive probability distribution map. The approach also uses a Bayesian χ^2 test for goodness-of-fit and goes on to show that the model closely fits a synthetic dataset. Reference [4] provides a study of missing person behavior in Australia, conducted by Victoria Police. The study, which is part of the SARBayes project, considers a large dataset of parameters, some of which have more significance than others.

Terrain plays an important role and the range of activities, relating to the missing person, are also considered (e.g. climbing, canoeing, hunting).

2.2 Machine learning and formal approaches

There are also several other machine learning-related approaches for dealing with missing person cases. For example, [5] compares the use of neural networks and rule-based systems for missing person cases in Australia. In later work [6] considers the use of J48 to derive rules, based on the popular C4.5 decision tree generator.

In the author's own previous work [7] a missing person model was developed based on Situation Calculus. The approach represented the state changes that take place over time, whilst missing. The formalisms help to provide a consistent means to represent the uncertainty present in such investigations.

2.3 Empirical approaches

Two widely accepted empirical approaches are those of the UK booklet 'Missing Persons: Understanding, Planning and Responding' (colloquially referred to as the Grampian Study) [8] and the iFIND System [9], which is currently used by a number of UK Police forces.

The Grampian Study considers a similar set of at-risk groups to that of the author's work. For each group the study provides a number of tables, which portray useful information, such as likely time periods of missing, distance traveled and likely places where a misper could be found. The Grampian Study also translates data into useful search ranges that can be superimposed on a map (**Figure 2**).

iFIND follows a similar structure but is based on more recent data to provide more thorough coverage. iFIND provides more detail in terms of possible locations. Both Grampian and iFIND place emphasis on Time, Distance and Likely Location and these parameters also feature predominantly in the author's work. **Figure 3** shows a typical excerpt from iFIND in the form of a table, which highlights the places where mispers for the category were located. The majority are found outside

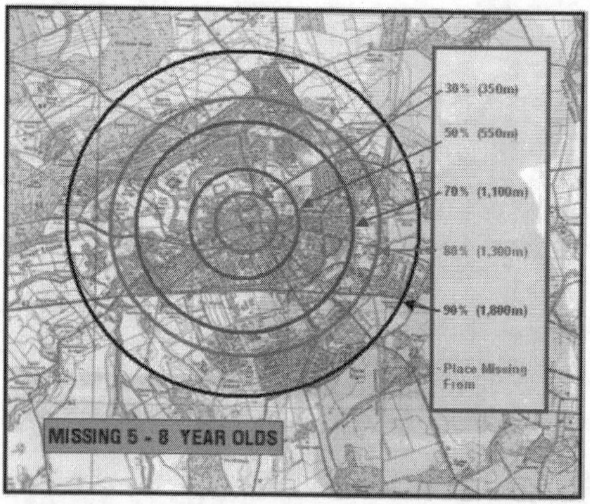

Figure 2.
Grampian search profiles for 5–8 year olds.

	Where located	Further information
37%	Outside in local area	Streets; parks; shops; fields.
18%	Returned to home address	Mostly playing with friends in the local area either on the street or at a friend's address; one had played in a park; another played in a woodland area alone.
	At a friend's	Playing.
8%	Went to home address	Mostly from school; others mainly from a street or shops.
5%	Found on premises	Playing or hiding.
3%	Home of a family member	Usually grandparents (where mentioned).
	At a public building	Local shops.
1%	Returned to school	Walking the streets in local area alone before returning.
	Pub	One was playing pool with his brother; another was taken to pub by grandmother.
Individual cases	Woodland	Had become lost.
	In vehicle elsewhere	Playing with a friend within a parked vehicle on a neighbour's drive.
	Bus station	Had been at an older boy's house overnight.

Figure 3.
iFIND table of likely locations for 5–8 year olds.

locally, with a smaller proportion either returning home or being found at a friend's house.

2.4 Geospatial approaches

Other research conducted by the author led to the development of the CASPER System (Computer Assisted Search Prioritization and Environmental Response) [10] to study the Geographies of Missing Persons. CASPER used primary and applied research and secondary data analysis to develop a Google map application to assist investigative and strategic decision-making. CASPER was developed to a prototype stage and demonstrated to several Police forces as a viable alternative to existing case management systems COMPACT [11] and NICHE [12] systems.

CASPER (**Figure 4**) was rich in terms of the geospatial information it provided, being able to display heatmaps, places of interest and even live CCTV footage. CASPER allows the search team to overlay a range of different layers onto a map region of interest. For example, the team may choose to overlay information on ATM cash machines if it is known that a misper is short of money. Alternatively, suicide hotspots can be overlaid (from precompiled suicide data) when dealing with a potential suicide case.

However, the algorithms used in CASPER were largely rule-based, developed from 'people like you' approaches, based on *if-elseif-else* structures.

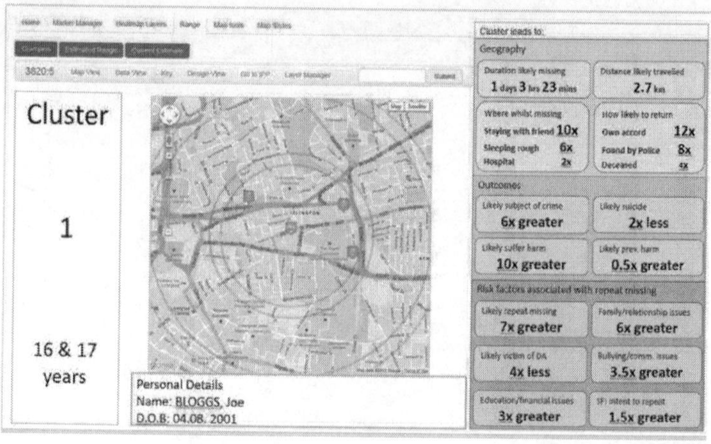

Figure 4.
CASPER missing persons prototype.

3. Bayesian network theory

BNs are directed graphical models that have been used extensively in the fields of cognitive science and artificial intelligence throughout the latter half of the 20th and early 21st centuries. The models are based on the theorem of Thomas Bayes [13], which allow probabilities to be updated in light of new evidence. BNs have been used for some time within the AI community and more recently amongst the machine learning community. Reference [14] provides an excellent account of how probability theory and decision theory began to attract the attention of the AI community in the late 1980s, which, when combined with graph theory, led to what we refer to today as Bayesian Networks.

Formally, for a discrete random variable $X = \{X_1, \cdots, X_n\}$, a BN is an annotated directed acyclic graph, which encodes a joint probability distribution (JPD) over X. Formally, a BN can be expressed as the pair $N = \langle G, \Theta \rangle$. The first element in N, is a directed acyclic graph, $G = (V, E)$. V denotes the random variables in X, and E denotes the edges, which represent direct dependencies between the variables. The second element Θ denotes the set of parameters, which quantify the network, via conditional probability tables. Each node is annotated with a conditional probability distribution, $P(X_i \mid \boldsymbol{Pa}(X_i))$, representing the conditional probability of the node X_i given its parents in G. The network N defines a unique JPD over X given by:

$$P(X_1, \cdots, X_n) = \prod_{i=1}^{N} P(X_i \mid \boldsymbol{Pa}(X_i)) \quad (1)$$

In a BN, a *conditional* probability $P(X \,/\, Y)$ is the probability of an event X occurring given that Y occurs. A *marginal* probability is effectively an unconditional probability. A marginal probability is a distribution formed by calculating the subset of a larger probability distribution. For example, given a JPD $P(X, Y)$ to determine the probability of X all the values for X = *False* and X = *True* can be summed in the joint table. When a node is queried in a BN, the result is often referred to as the *marginal* for that node.

For BNs, inference, is the computational method for deriving answers to queries given a probability model expressed as a BN. Inference in BNs can take on several different forms [15, 16], broadly speaking, it may be exact or approximate, depending upon the structure of the graph. Exact inference is not always possible when the number of combinations and paths is excessively large. However, it is often possible to refactor a BN graph (i.e. alter the graph structure) before resorting to approximate inference.

Let U be the set of random variables. Let $U^e \subseteq U$ be the set of known (evidence) variables. Let $X^q \in U \setminus U^e$ be the variables of interest (queries) and let $U^r = U \setminus (U^e \cup X^q)$ be the set of remaining variables.

The probability distribution of the evidence variables and the query variables via marginalization, can be calculated as:

$$P(X^q, U^e) = \sum_{U^r} P(X_1, \cdots, X_N) \tag{2}$$

The normalization may be calculated as:

$$P(U^e) = \sum_{U^q} P(X^q, U^e) \tag{3}$$

Then conditional probabilities may be calculated as:

$$P(X^q \mid U^e) = \frac{P(X^q, U^e)}{P(U^e)} \tag{4}$$

A range of different questions can be asked, via inference, in relation to the probability distribution, such as:

- Diagnosis: *P(X = cause | U = symptom)*
- Prediction: *P(X = symptom | U = cause)*
- Classification: *max P(X = class | U = data)*
- class
- Decision-making (given a cost function)

The different questions may be considered in relation to how classical statistical models help to estimate either the value of something - regression framework or the state of something - classification framework. Prediction and classification would be as per the classical statistical model framework. Diagnosis adds to this by defining the outcomes from the model in organizational terms (e.g. Policing terms, such as high priority cases). Decision-making adds further to this by using the diagnosis to guide Policing activities. Decision-making effectively translates the statistical model into operational terminology for operational decision-making.

Essentially, a BN defines a unique JPD over *X* and computationally the JPD takes the form of a large table, constructed from the tables defined at individual nodes, in accordance with the graph links. So computationally, inference is the process of scanning the joint table to find a value (or values), which correspond to evidence E, possibly summing values along the way. Often, the table will take the form of a sparse matrix and this property can be exploited to make inference tractable, even when the number of parameters is very large. There are certain legal rearrangements of the JPD table in which certain parameters can be marginalized.

Such rearrangements allow queries to be satisfied in linear-time methods by identifying a subgraph of the original graph relevant to the query [17].

4. Misper-Bayes model for missing person investigations

The Misper-Bayes model was developed from previous research conducted by the author [1]. The model represents the different categories of at-risk missing persons and their breakdown in terms of sex type and age. The model also represents the likely times that a person may be missing, and the distance traveled as well as the likely locations where they may be found. Data from iFIND was used to determine the male/female split and the same set of at-risk categories as iFIND were adopted. All of the iFIND data was examined and a set of network parameters were compiled.

The Misper-Bayes model is shown below (**Figure 5**) in terms of a digraph and associated conditional probability tables. The nodes in the graph represent the random variables, which are linked through the conditional probability tables. Most of the tables are fairly self-explanatory, with a couple of exceptions: the Cat(x) table reflects the different categories of at-risk mispers and the Loc(x) table reflects the different locations where mispers are likely to be found. Note that there is no edge connecting Cat(x) and Time(x) (although there was an edge in an earlier version of the model). It was found that Age(x) provides a better predictor of the time spend missing than Cat(x). For example, the age of a young child or an elderly subject has a direct bearing on the time that they are missing. Other variables were included in earlier versions of the model, such as race or ethnicity, but these were seen to have a lesser effect than the variables shown in **Figure 5**.

Recalling Eq. (1), which gives the JPD over X given as:

$$P(X_1, \cdots X_n) = \prod_{i=1}^{N} P(X_i \mid \boldsymbol{Pa}(X_i))$$

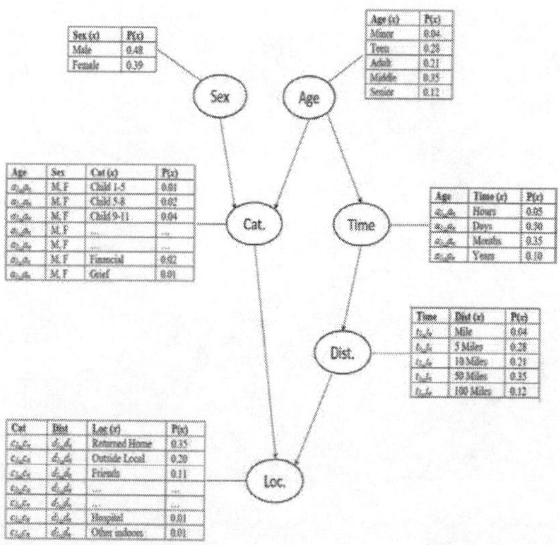

Figure 5.
Misper-Bayes model.

The Misper-Bayes graphical model can be written as:

$$P(L,D,C,T,S,A) = P(L \mid D,C)\, P(D \mid T)\, P(C \mid S,A)\, P(T \mid A)\, P(S)\, P(A) \quad (5)$$

where:
$P(A)$ is the probability of the different age groups.
$P(S)$ is the probability of the sex types male and female.
$P(T \mid A)$ is the conditional probability of time missing, based on age.
$P(C \mid S, A)$ is the conditional probability of the different categories, based on sex type and age group.
$P(D \mid T)$ is the conditional probability of distance traveled, based on time missing.
$P(L \mid D, C)$ is the conditional probability of the likely location, based on the different categories and the distance traveled.

Software libraries are available for common programming languages, which can be used to implement BNs. Two popular libraries for the Python programming language are pomegranate [18] and bnlearn [19]. bnlearn is a library, which can be used to learn the structure of a BN and estimate the parameters, based on a dataset [20]. bnlearn was used in this instance to learn the network structure based on data from iFIND. After several iterations and variable eliminations, the development process arrived at a graph similar to **Figure** 5. bnlearn starts with an empty network structure of all variables, then proceeds by adding, removing and reversing edges between nodes to maximize the goodness of fit of the model. The final structure, learned by bnlearn, contained an excessive number of edges, likely due to overfitting (i.e. noise within the data had been represented in the model itself). The unnecessary edges were thinned out, based on the interpretation of the causal relationships between variables to deliver the final structure of **Figure 5**. Finally, bnlearn was used to learn the parameters using iFIND data compiled from the summary table (**Figure 3**).

The model was trialed using a series of realistic misper cases and the results were promising (approx.. 90% agreement) in relation to those of iFIND. A full set of the results are available in [1].

5. Conclusions

The chapter has described the design and implementation of the Misper-Bayes model, which can be used to assist Police forces in determining the whereabouts of a missing person. Misper-Bayes provides a powerful tool, which can be used to good effect to whittle down the likely locations where the missing person may be found. The Misper-Bayes model was evaluated using a series of queries with a set of misper cases. For each query, the results of the model were cross-checked against the results of the iFIND system and the accuracy was approx.. 90%. The strength of the model lies in its simplicity yet versatility. When combined with a geospatial front-end (e.g. CASPER) [21–23], the Misper-Bayes model can be used to very good effect to assist Police Officers with the prioritization of their search strategy. The approach has also demonstrated the scope of BNs to support evidence-based policing beyond that of missing person cases.

References

[1] Reilly D, Taylor M, Fergus P, Chalmers C, Thompson S. Misper-Bayes: A Bayesian network model for missing person investigations. IEEE Access. 2021;**9**:49990-50000

[2] Stone LD, Keller CM, Kratzke TM, Strumpfer JP. Search for the wreckage of air France flight AF 447. Statistical Science. 2014;**29**(1):69-80

[3] Lin L, Goodrich MA. A Bayesian approach to modeling lost person behaviors based on terrain features in wilderness search and rescue. Computational and Mathematical Organization Theory. 2010;**16**:300-323

[4] Sava E, Twardy C, Koester R, Sonwalkar M. Evaluating lost person behavior models. Transactions in GIS. 2016;**20**(1):38-53

[5] Blackmore K, Bossomaier T, Foy S, Thomson D. Data mining of missing persons data. In: Proc. 1st International Conference on Fuzzy Systems and Knowledge Discovery: Computational Intelligence for the E-Age, Singapore. Berlin, Heidelberg: Springer; 2002

[6] Blackmore K, Boosomaier T. Comparison of See5 and J48: PART algorithms for missing person profiling. In: Proc. 1st International Conference on Information Technology and Applications, ICITA 1–6, Australia. 2002

[7] Taylor MJ, Reilly D. Knowledge representation for missing persons investigations. Journal of Systems and Information Technology. 2017;**19**(2): 138-150

[8] Gibb G, Woolnough P. Missing Persons: Understanding, Planning, Responding – A Guide for Police Officers. Aberdeen: Grampian Police; 2017. Available from: http://www.searchresearch.org.uk/downloads/ukmpbs/GGIbb_missing_person_report.pdf

[9] N. Eales. "iFIND", National Crime Agency (NCA), London, UK [Online]. 2015. Available from: https://missingpersons.police.uk/en-gb/resources/downloads/iFIND

[10] Reilly D, Wren C, Giles S, Cunnigham L, Hargreaves P. CASPER: Computer assisted search prioritisation and environmental response application. In: Proc. Sixth International Conference on Developments Is E-Systems Engineering (DeSE'06), Abu Dhabi, UAE. IEEE; 2013. pp. 225-230

[11] WPC Software. COMPACT. Available from: https://www.wpcsoft.com/business-areas/compact

[12] NicheRMS. [Online]. Available from: https://nicherms.com/products

[13] Stone JV. Bayes Rule: A Tutorial Introduction to Bayesian Analysis. Sebtel Press; 2013. ISBN 978-0-9563728-4-0

[14] D'Ambrosio B. Inference in Bayesian networks. AI Magazine. 1999; **20**(2):21

[15] Darwiche A. Modelling and Reasoning with Bayesian Networks. Cambridge: Cambridge University Press; 2009

[16] Larranaga P, Karshenas H, Bielza C, Santana R. A review on evolutionary algorithms in Bayesian network learning and inference tasks. Elsevier Information Sciences. 2013;**233**:109-125

[17] Geiger D, Verma T, Pearl J. d-separation: From theorems to algorithms. In: Proc. Fifth Workshop Uncertainty in Artificial Intelligence, Ontario, Canada. 1989. pp. 118-125

[18] Schreiber J. Pomegranate: Fast and flexible probabilistic modeling in

python. Journal of Machine Learning Research. 2018;**18**(164):1-6

[19] bnlearn – Graphical structure of Bayesian networks [Online]. Available from: https://pypi.org/project/bnlearn

[20] National Crime Agency. 2017. Missing Person Data Report 2015/2016. [Online]. Available from: http://missing persons.police.uk/en-gb/resources/ downloads/missing-person-statistical-bulletins

[21] Uusitalo L. Advantages and challenges of Bayesian networks in environmental modelling. Ecological Modelling. 2007;**203**:312-318

[22] Kyrimi E, Mossadegh S, Tai N, Marsh W. An incremental explanation of inference in Bayesian networks for increasing model trustworthiness and supporting clinical decision making. Artificial Intelligence in Medicine. 2020; **103**. ISSN 0933-3657

[23] McLachlan S, Dube K, Hitman GA, Fenton NE, Kyrimi E. Bayesian networks in healthcare: Distribution by medical condition. Artificial Intelligence in Medicine. 2020;**107**, ISSN 0933-3657

Chapter 4

The Applicability of Internet Voting in Africa

Abstract

The covid-19 pandemic has brought about new ways of conducting business through the use of Information Communication Technologies and elections have not been spared either. Internet voting is another form of strengthening democracy through the use of Information Communication Technologies. Africa lags in the implementation of electronic voting, especially Internet voting. This chapter applied a critical socio-technical analysis that analyses factors that influence the applicability of Internet voting within the African context. The researcher applied desktop research which included 30 journals to gather data from the Internet and other documentation sources. The findings reveal that decision-makers can partially implement Internet voting in some of the countries in Africa like Kenya, Libya, Nigeria, Morocco, Mauritius, Tunisia, and Seychelles. To successfully implement Internet voting, the decision-makers in African nations have to fully invest in the Information Communication Technology infrastructure, provide the necessary security, legislation and carry out intensive voter education to build trust among voters.

Keywords: Covid-19, lockdown, pandemic, Internet voting, critical socio-technical analysis, democracy

1. Introduction

Democracy has formed the foundation of governance in the world, with every voter willing to express his/her views on the ballot [1, 2]. Elections have been held manually and electronically in both the developed and developing nations, some results have ended in contestations and wars erupting after the elections. Covid-19 has had a devastating effect on the political, social, and economic spheres in the world [3]. The way of running elections was also affected by this pandemic as nations sought to find ways of halting the spread of the disease. In developed nations countries like Estonia and other American states have been implementing Internet voting.

Africa is constituted by 54 countries with diversified democracies [4]. Eritrea is the only country that does not hold regular elections as has continuously postponed elections citing security threat from its neighbors Ethiopia and Djibouti. The African nations have diversified electoral systems, with some countries like Zimbabwe implementing first past the post and proportional representation, and South Africa, the proportional representation in their polls [5]. Most of the African countries hold regular manual elections as demanded by the United Nations Universal Declarations on elections.

The prospects for the growth of democracy in the 21st century in Africa depend on how the continent positions itself for value-adding services such as

Internet voting. Covid –19 has forced the world to quickly develop and implement Information Communication Technologies (ICT) opportunities previously unimaginable. For Africa to take advantage of this, an effective enabling environment and use of ICTs is a particularly important contributor to modern democracy.

2. Literature review

Internet voting is where a ballot is cast by the voter through the Internet [6]. The use of Internet voting gained popularity in Estonia since 2001. Estonia is the first country to carry out a successful pilot project in municipal elections in 2005. Estonia went on further to first use Internet voting in the 2007 parliamentary elections [7].

The four kinds of Internet voting are kiosk Internet voting, polling-place Internet voting, precinct Internet voting, and remote Internet voting (Canada-Europe Transatlantic [8]). Kiosk Internet voting involves the use of a computer at a specific location (an authorized internet polling station) that is controlled by election officials. This differs from a standalone electronic voting machine because the ballot is immediately transmitted over the Internet to the central vote-counting site. Polling-place Internet voting is conducted through the use of a computer at any polling station and is supervised by the usual election officials. Precinct Internet voting is very similar to polling-place voting except that it must occur at the voter's designated precinct polling station (voters are only allowed to cast their ballots at polling stations where they are registered). Remote Internet voting is where a voter cast the ballot from the comfort of their homes or where the is Internet provision [9]. The advantages, disadvantages, and countries that are implementing Internet voting are shown in **Table 1**.

Internet Voting type	Advantages	Disadvantages	Countries implementing the system
1. Remote Internet voting	• Convenient and accessible for voters who have Internet access at home, at work, or abroad; and for persons with disabilities, the military, single parents, voters who are traveling, etc. • Flexible voting time for voters • Flagging of ballot errors • Replication of ballot images without voter information for counting or audit purposes • Lower cost than traditional methods • Potential to enhance electoral efficiency • Faster and more accurate election results • Elimination of long queues • Instant absentee ballot • Font size and screen language can be modified	• Limited access to the Internet or limited understanding on part of some voters • Possibility of stolen voter packages or identification cards • Misuse of voter's Identity Card (ID) and personal information voting by others without the knowledge of the voter • Difficulty verifying voter ID • Possible pressure on voters to vote a certain way if in the presence of others • Hacks or viruses attacking the systems and altering election results • Technical difficulties, programming errors, or server malfunctions • Inaccuracies of the voter's list, resulting in one voter receiving a card intended for another voter	Australia (for military and persons with disabilities only), Austria, Canada, Estonia, Netherlands, Switzerland, USA (for the military-), UK (project canceled)

Internet Voting type	Advantages	Disadvantages	Countries implementing the system
2. Kiosk Internet voting	• Placement inconvenient high traffic locations (for example, malls and supermarkets) • Flexible voting time for voters • Flagging of ballot errors • Replication of ballot images without voter information for counting or audit purposes • Potential to help address the voting needs of certain groups of voters (persons with disabilities, single parents, etc) • Potential to enhance electoral efficiency • Faster and more accurate election results • Elimination of long queues	• Lack of paper trail to allow auditing and recounts • In the case of a power outage, no alternate method is available • Cost of machines • Software may sometimes be unreliable • Voters may leave the voting screen before the ballot is officially cast • Hacks or viruses attacking the system and altering results • Voters may be pressured to vote a certain way if in the presence of others • Technical difficulties, programming errors, server malfunctions • Machine updating and cost • Candidate representative's oversight function may be diminished • Inaccuracies on the voters' list could result in one voter receiving a card intended for another voter	France
3. Polling place Internet voting	• Eliminates mismarked or spoiled ballots and other invalid results • Programmable machines to dispense ballots for any election • Removal of authentication questions so voter identification is most similar to the traditional process • Assistive devices to improve accessibility for voters with disabilities • Faster and accurate election results • Font size and screen language can be modified	• Auditing and recounts can be questioned if there is no paper trail • In the case of a machine failure (that is, power outage) no alternate method is available • Cost of machines • Software may sometimes be unreliable (many machines have a negative reputation based on failure in USA trials) • Voters may leave the voting screen before the ballot is officially cast • Little advantage for voters in terms of convenience • Machine updating could also be an issue and costly	Australia, Belgium, Brazil, Canada, Finland, France, Germany, India, Ireland Netherlands, Norway, Portugal, Spain, Switzerland, United Kingdom, United States of America

Internet Voting type	Advantages	Disadvantages	Countries implementing the system
4. Precinct Internet voting	• Elimination of mismarked or spoiled ballots and other invalid results • Programmable machines to dispense ballots for any election • Assistive devices to improve accessibility for voters with disabilities • Removal of authentication questions so that voter identification is most similar to the traditional process • Faster and accurate election results • Font and screen language can be modified	• Auditing and recounts can be questioned if there is no paper trail • In the case of machine failure (that is power outage), no alternate is available • Machines are expensive • The software can sometimes be unreliable • A voter may leave a voting screen before the ballot has been officially cast • Little additional convenience for voters • Machine updating could also be costly	
5. Telephone/ Mobile/ Voice over Internet Protocol (VOIP)	• Convenience and accessibility for voters who have telephones or mobile gadgets; and for certain groups of voters (persons with disabilities, military, single parents, travelers, etc. • Flexible voting time for voters • Flagging of ballot errors • Familiar technology, especially for those familiar with telephone banking • No ballot printing • Fewer elections staff and poll locations • Less costly • Potential increase in voter turnout • Enhanced electoral efficiency • Elimination of long queues	• No paper trail makes traditional recount impossible • Possibility of stolen voter packages or identification cards • Difficulty verifying voter ID • Must ensure candidate representative's function is written into the program (e.g. Halifax candidate module) • Others present may pressure voters to vote a certain way • Possible telephone/mobile lines overloading or phone service interruption • Inaccuracies on the voter' list could result in one voter receiving a card intended for another voter	Netherlands, United Kingdom

Source: Sambo [10].

Table 1.
Comparison of internet voting methods.

As shown in **Table 1**, Internet voting is necessitated by the demographics of a country especially people living abroad who would want to exercise their democratic right but will not be residing within the citizenry country during an election. Chisinau [11] argues that Internet voting will allow voters to cast their ballots at the comfort of their homes or convenient places. Voting through the Internet is easier as voters can cast ballots using their own devices and there is no time wasted in long queues. Voters do not travel long distances, thus reducing transportation costs and can do other business chores. It allows for inclusivity as people living with disabilities or serious medical conditions can exercise their democratic rights. Internet voting will also allow those people who will be traveling or will be on duty during election day to cast their ballots anywhere in the world [12].

The disadvantage of Internet voting is that it consists of a large complex network which makes it difficult to monitor the entire network, thus posing a serious security threat. The monitoring of the network is very expensive of which there is no 100 percent guarantee that the network will be secure. Hackers could use malware to rig the outcome of the elections, by tampering with the way votes are submitted and counted or even casting votes for people who did not vote. Internet voting may be a source of conflict between political parties if one party considers that Internet voting might be beneficial to the other party/parties [12].

2.1 Critical socio-technical analysis

The critical socio-technical analysis [10] which is premised on analyzing an information system during the systems development life cycle was used to identify key factors in the applicability of Internet voting in Africa. By finding key factors affecting the applicability of Internet voting in Africa, it is expected that decision-makers would come up with strategies that support the successful implementation of such systems.

African Electoral Management Bodies (EMBs) have been using manual systems in general elections for the past decades which has resulted in disputed elections, high operating costs affecting the Gross Domestic Product (GDP) because of systems and processes inefficiency. Only two countries, the Democratic Republic of Congo and Namibia have used polling stationed-based electronic voting machines which do not have Internet connectivity [13]. Covid-19 has not helped the situation either as countries have been forced into lockdowns, compelling nations to postpone elections. The introduction of Internet voting especially casting a ballot outside a polling station is the most difficult technological upgrade for an Electoral Management Body (EMB) as it involves the core of the entire electoral process [14]. This chapter investigated 'why' and 'what' factors were affecting the applicability of Internet voting in African general elections.

3. Methodology

In this study, desktop research was used to collect data from 30 journals and other documentation about factors affecting the applicability of Internet voting in Africa. The critical socio-technical analysis was then used to guide this study in the search and analysis of factors such as political, social, technical, legal, security, privacy, trust, and transparency affecting the applicability of Internet voting in Africa. These factors were selected after critically analyzing contemporary issues in developing and developed countries successfully implementing, on trials or have abandoned the implementation of Internet voting.

4. Findings

While the benefits from Internet voting will guarantee the rights of citizens to exercise their democratic rights, the study discovered that no country in Africa is implementing Internet voting in general elections. The factors affecting the applicability of Internet voting in Africa are political, legal, social, technical, security, privacy, transparency, and trust.

4.1 Political

Africa has the most number of people that flee their countries seeking greater opportunities from developing and developed nations [15]. Citizens from African countries migrate to other countries due to the effects of climatic changes, such as droughts, storms, and flooding. Other factors such as economic and political stability (wars) also force nationals to migrate to other countries seeking better opportunities [16]. The migration of people allows African countries to offer their citizens their democratic rights by allowing them to vote through the Internet. Some African governments also tend Internet shutdowns citing national security or curbing the spread of fake news during elections, for example, the Ugandan, Libya, Malawi, and Sudan Presidential elections [17] which makes it difficult to implement Internet voting.

4.1.1 Legal

The legal framework allows voters to exercise their rights during an election or absentee voting through the Internet [18]. For African citizens living abroad or who will be committed during election day to exercise their democratic right, there must be legislation that supports Internet voting. The legal framework empowers the EMB and other stakeholders to remove the element of mistrust, as the voting process is done within the confines of the law. At the moment no country in Africa is exploring the use of Internet voting rendering the introduction of such legislation a futile exercise.

4.1.2 Technical

African countries are still facing challenges in the implementation of mobile communication and Internet technologies [19]. Countries like Somalia, South Sudan, and Mozambique have often been affected by ravaging wars, which destroys infrastructure and forcing these countries into retarded economic growth. As shown in **Table 1**, the limitation in the Internet penetration factor is that the network service providers do not provide 100% service coverage. This makes it practically impossible to offer Internet voting within the country for national general elections as some other communities will be disadvantaged by failing to access the service to cast their ballots. The penetration of internet communication in Africa is very low at 43% as shown in **Table 2**. Countries like Kenya, Libya, Mauritius, Nigeria, Morocco, Seychelles, and Tunisia have a higher national Internet penetration factor. These countries can partially implement Internet voting in some of their regions. Other African nations especially that are below 50% like Eretria, Togo, Western Sahara, South Sudan, Sierra Leone, and Somalia will have difficulties in implementing Internet voting nationally.

4.1.3 Social

There is a wide gap between the digital divide within the African nations especially between the urban and the rural community, the elderly, and the young generations [20]. The young generations have embraced technology as they use smartphones and laptops as communication and business tools. A large population in African countries live in rural communities. Some of these people cannot afford to buy gadgets, power, and data used for Internet services. There is also a lack of digital skills and literacy among the communities both in urban and rural setups especially among the elderly. The content or language used on the Internet makes it difficult for some African communities to comprehend the importance of using such services. Hence the use of Internet voting in African countries will be difficult because of the digital divide.

4.1.4 Security

Internet voting should be secure for the results to be credible [21]. Key factors such as freedom, and equality during an election are important aspects of security

Country	Estimated Population	Estimated Registered Voters	Estimated Voter population	Internet Users 31 December 2020	Penetration (% Population)
Algeria	44,616,624	24,474,161	27,992,084	25,428,159	57.0%
Angola	33,933,610	4,992,399	5,967,849	8,980,670	26.5%
Benin	12,451,040	4,802,303	5,378,554	3,801,758	30.5%
Botswana	2,397,241	924,709	1,444,142	1,139,000	47.5%
Burkina Faso	21, 497,096	2,395,226	2,497,500	4,594,625	21.4%
Burundi	12,255,433	5,113,418	5,863,257	1,606,122	13.1%
Cabo Verde	561,898	392,731	N/A	352,120	62.7%
Cameroon	27,224,265	6,900,928	13,001,295	7,878,422	28.9%
Central African Rep.	4,919,981	1,954,433	2,005,942	557,085	11.3%
Chad	16,914,985	6,252,548	5,809,346	2,237,932	13.2%
Comoros	888,451	313,647	474,387	193,700	21.8%
Congo	5,657,013	2,221,596	2,617,983	833,200	14.7%
Congo Dem. Rep.	92,377,993	40,371,439	44,138,661	16,355,917	17.7%
Cote d'Ivoire	27,053,629	7,359,399	15,503,401	12,253,653	45.3%
Djiboti	1,002,187	215,687	609,344	548,832	54.8%
Egypt	104,258,327	63,157,351	63,705,978	54,741,493	52.5%
Equatorial Guinea	1,449,896	325,555	417,365	362,891	25.0%
Eritrea	3,601,467	N/A	N/A	248,199	6.9%
Eswatini	1,172,362	546,784	N/A	665,245	56.7%
Ethiopia	117,876,227	36,851,461	49,011,364	21,147,255	17.9%
Gabon	2,278,825	680,194	1,177,350	1,367,641	60.0%
Gambia	2,486,945	886,578	1,151,645	442,050	19.0%
Ghana	31,732,129	17,027,641	N/A	14,767,818	46.5%
Guinea	13,497,244	5,410,089	6,556,813	2,551,672	18.9%
Guinea-Bissau	2,015,494	645,085	935,920	250,000	12.4%
Kenya	54,985,698	15,590,236	25,374,082	46,870,422	85.2%
Lesotho	2,159,079	1,254,506	N/A	682,990	31.6%
Liberia	5,180,203	2,183,629	2,319,382	760,994	14.7%
Libya	6,958,532	1,509,218	4,029,365	5,857,000	84.2%
Madagascar	28,427,328	10,302,194	14,291,036	2,864,000	10.1%
Malawi	19,647,684	6,859,570	10,030,988	2,717,243	13.8%
Mali	20,855,735	7,663,464	8,920,714	12,480,176	59.8%
Mauritania	4,775,119	1,417,823	2,125,242	969,519	20.3%
Mauritius	1,273,433	941,719	1,044,325	919,000	72.2%
Mayotee (FR)	279,515	N/A	N/A	107,940	38.6%
Morocco	37,344,795	15,702,592	23,126,996	25,589,581	68.5%
Mozambique	32,163,047	13,153,088	13,554,684	6,523,613	20.3%
Namibia	2,587,344	1,358,468	1,479,603	1,347,418	52.11%
Niger	25,130,817	7,446,556	9,623,301	3,363,848	13.4%
Nigeria	211,400,708	82,344,107	106,490,312	154,301,195	73.0%
Reunion (FR)	901,686	110,968	N/A	608,000	67.4%
Rwanda	13,276,513	7,172,612	N/A	5,981,638	45.1%
Saint Helena (UK)	6,086	2,309	N/A	2,300	37.8%

Country	Estimated Population	Estimated Registered Voters	Estimated Voter population	Internet Users 31 December 2020	Penetration (% Population)
Sao Tome & Princepe	223,368	97,274	105,318	63,684	28.6%
Senegal	17,196,301	6,683,043	8,071,074	9,749,527	56.7%
Seychelles	98,908	74,634	N/A	71,300	72.1%
Sierra Leone	8,141,343	3,178,663	3,284,182	1,043,725	12.8%
Somalia	16,359,504	4,220,466	N/A	2,089,900	12.8%
South Africa	60,041,994	25,809,443	37,372,792	34,545,165	57.5%
South Sudan	11,381,378	4,800,000	N/A	900,716	7.9%
Sudan	44,909,353	13,126,989	19,667,400	13,124,100	29.2%
Tanzania	61,498,437	29,754,699	29,480,237	23,142,960	37.6%
Togo	8,478,437	3,738,786	4,645,140	1,011,837	11.9%
Tunisia	11,935,766	7,065,885	8,219,612	8,170,000	68.4%
Uganda	47,123,531	8,219,612	8,219,612	18,502,166	39.3%
Western Sahara	611,875	N/A	N/A	28,000	4.6%
Zambia	18,920,651	6,698,372	7,331,669	9,870,427	52.2%
Zimbabwe	15,092,171	5,695,706	7,650,931	8,400,000	55.7%
Total Africa	1,373,486,514			590,296,163	43.0%
Rest of world	6,502,279,070	N/A	N/A	4,463,594,959	68.6%
World Total	7,875,765,584			5,053,891,122	64.2%

Source:https://www.internetworldstats.com/stats1.htm, https://www.idea.int/data-tools/continent-view/Africa/40

Table 2.
Internet users statistics for Africa.

requirements for Internet voting. The transmission of all voting data to servers or tabulation centers must be secure. All voting which is done whether on the Internet or otherwise should be granted the same status as any other vote cast in the same election. This means that each vote should be given the same weight as it also determines the outcome of an election [22]. Various encryption methods have been suggested for use with Internet voting including the blockchain [23]. African countries should have networks that can encrypt ballots cast over the Internet without the network being compromised, overloaded, or due to other disruptions like shutdowns.

4.1.5 Privacy

With the use of Internet voting, an EMB has to ensure that each vote cast remains a secret. A free election means that the voter must not be coerced by public or private pressure. After voting through the Internet, the voters should have an acknowledgment for the candidate that they have voted for. All ballots cast through the Internet should be accorded the same secrecy as in manual systems [24]. If a ballot is cast, the voter's identification details must be able to be authenticated and not linked to the ballot. The vote cast should also be accounted for in the outcome without identifying the voter. In Africa voter intimidation remains a serious challenge [25], thus through Internet voting, voters may be coerced to vote for undeserving candidates.

4.1.6 Trust and transparency

Trust in Internet voting can only be accepted if the results from this service are credible. The EMB should assure voters that their votes are secure and secret. To build trust voters should also be able to verify that all collected ballots were from eligible voters and that they have been accurately counted [26]. If Internet voting is to be implemented in African countries pilot testing has to be undertaken to allow voters to test the system before being fully implemented in a general election. To build trust among stakeholders (voters, activists, and media) an EMB should be transparent in all the activities involved with Internet voting. To avoid mistrust from the public, the stakeholders should be educated on how Internet voting works and also made to appreciate the qualities of the system. Relevant information should be availed in a language that can easily be understood by the public. The information should include full technical documentation of how the system is designed functionally and technically, all levels of software documentation, source code, and the technical and organizational environments where the system is hosted.

4.2 Discussion and analysis

With the advent of the Covid-19 pandemic causing deaths, and unavoidable shutdowns, elections cannot be suspended indefinitely, decision-makers have to find alternative ways of conducting elections without compromising the health and safety of the electorate. Internet voting is one such method that may guarantee the health and safety of the electorate where voters can vote in the comfort of their homes. Decision-makers have to take note of the following during feasibility studies and implementation of Internet voting:

Politically, it is fundamental to foster a broad consensus among political parties for the implementation of Internet voting. This involves transparency where the relevant actors have a voice. Internet voting should be seen as politically neutral that is the new procedure should not benefit disproportionally given factions of the political spectrum [27]. For electoral results to be accepted by voters, Internet voting must produce an outcome that reflects the will of the people in an environment that establishes transparency and trust [14].

Technological and security concerns are often pointed to as the main concern of Internet voting [28]. To validate and verify the technological voting system the set of technological requirements have to be consulted systematically. In Africa, some voters live in remote areas but may also want to cast their ballots using the Internet. African countries have limited Internet infrastructure which should prompt governments to improve this area if its citizens are to benefit from Internet voting. The improvement on the infrastructure would also benefit an EMB during the voter registration process, as voters will be able to register through the Internet.

There have been numerous attacks of electronic voting systems over the Internet with the 2016 American Presidential election being the most contentious election of the decade [29]. The stakes of any general election are always high, which may create interests chief among them malicious actors-particularly in countries with specific geopolitical adversaries who may specifically create and deploy attacks or malware designed to manipulate the vote. In Africa, the use of Internet voting which has got limited transparency and audit trail may lead to manipulation and voter fraud. It will be very difficult to monitor votes cast over the Internet, to build trust among the citizens an EMB has to be trusted in pursuing its mandate.

Most electronic voting systems are now being developed with blockchain encryption [30, 31]. Blockchain technology is an end-to-end encryption method that secures ballots transmitted from voters' private devices to a centralized tabulation facility. However, it has been observed that most serious vulnerabilities threatening integrity and secrecy of voting happen before ballots ever reach the blockchain. Voters may be coerced by family members or other pressure groups to vote in a certain way that does not reflect their will. It is also difficult to validate if the voter is the real one casting the ballot which

Internet voting used in General Elections	Partial use of Internet voting and Special cases	Planned to be piloted or Piloted but Discontinued or Never Used
Estonia is the only country to allow citizens the option of online voting in local, national, and European elections	**Armenia:** Diplomatic staff and their families can vote online.	**France:** Voting was never used for out-of-country voters in the 2012 parliamentary elections but discontinued in 2017 due to security concerns; the government plans to bring it back in 2022. Out-of-country residents also voted online in the 2016 Republican party primaries.
	Australia: Online voting was trialed for out-of-country military personnel in 2017 but has been discontinued. New South Wales allows some groups- voters with disabilities, living in remote areas, out of state- to vote online, but there are no plans to extend this option to other states.	**India:** In 2010. Internet voting was trialed in the local elections in the state of Gujarat.
	Canada: Online voting is possible for municipal elections in some districts of Ontario and Nova Scotia. Canada has considered introducing Internet voting in federal elections.	**Norway:** Online voting for2011 local and 2013 national elections was made available in some districts. In 2014, Internet voting was discontinued for security reasons.
	Mexico: Some states have allowed online voting for out-of-sorts country voters.	In 2004, the **Netherlands** used Internet voting for an election to the *Rijnland* water board and in 2006 for out-of-country voters for national elections. Internet voting was discontinued in 2017 due to security concerns.
	New Zealand: Out-of-country voters can vote online.	**Spain:** In 2010, Barcelona held an online referendum on an urban development project. The voting was a one-off, online-only pilot and was highly controversial.
	Panama: Out-of-country voters can vote online.	**United Kingdom:** Online voting was trialed in local council elections between 2002 and 2007.
	Switzerland: Some cantons offer online voting to out-of-country voters- also in a few cases, to resident voters- in elections and referendums. The stated goal is to roll out Internet voting to the entire country.	**Russia:** is set to introduce its first online voting system. The system will be tested in a Moscow neighborhood that will elect a single member to the capital's city council in September 2019. One of the first experiments to introduce Internet voting was conducted by the Electoral Commission of the Volgograd Region during voting in Uryupinsk in 2009, and the Odintsovo district in 2010.
	United States: Despite the security concerns raised after a District of Columbia trial of Internet voting was hacked, more than 30 U.S. states allow military personnel and out-of-country residents to vote online. Voters using online or mail ballots waive their secrecy rights.	**Finland** has appointed a working group to study the technical feasibility of an online voting system. It determined that the technology does not yet sufficiently meet all the requirements, citing problems with reconciliation of verifiability and election secrecy

Source:http://www.europarl.europa.eu/RegData/etudes/BRIE/2018/625178/EPRS_BRI(2018)625178_E N.pdf

Table 3.
Countries that use internet voting (use of internet voting outside of polling stations in politically binding elections).

is crucial to the credibility of an election. Estonia, for instance, has resolved this issue without blockchain by using e-ID cards. Blockchain technology also does not protect against -denial-of-service attacks that make servers unable to operate, does not protect information as it travels on the Internet, and does not make servers and infrastructure more resistant to advanced persistent threats. Despite improvements in encryption techniques, security will always remain a challenge for Internet voting.

The major social challenge is the digital divide as some parts of the population remain excluded from Internet voting and that gap exists in African countries regarding computer literacy and household Internet usage and availability. The 'Digital transformation Strategy' adopted by African countries in February 2020 should be pursued to narrow the gap between the digital divide in urban and rural communities and also narrow the 'gender digital divide' [32].

Currently, most African countries do not have any legislation that supports Internet voting. The legal framework should be put in place to allow for Internet voting, which should clearly state who is eligible and the reasons that support eligibility.

Despite low usage in Internet voting around the world, Estonia is the only country that has fully utilized this service in general elections. **Table 3** highlights countries that have fully, partially, piloting and discontinued the use of Internet voting.

The success of Internet voting depends largely on how it is perceived by the people meant to use it: citizens. For example, Internet voting is difficult to be transparent as compared to manual systems. The transparency and reliability of Internet voting have been questioned, as this is electronically done. Therefore, it is fundamental to know what their attitudes towards the implementation of Internet voting would affect them.

5. Conclusions

The applicability of Internet voting in Africa largely depends on how the nation's willingness to adapt to new technology in the face of challenges such as political, legal, security, privacy, trust and transparency, the digital divide, and limited infrastructure. The successful experience of countries such as Estonia highlights the importance of a gradual, step-by-step design and implementation of Internet voting which may be used for benchmarking. It is also recommended that the perception of the citizens should be taken into consideration. African nations should also make an effort to improve the internal coverage of Internet services within their territories.

References

[1] Nwogu, G. A. . (2015). Democracy: Its Meaning and Dissenting Opinions of the Political Class in Nigeria: A Philosophical Approach. Journal of Education and Practice, *6*(32), 128-140. Retrieved from www.iiste.org

[2] Tar, U. (2010). The challenges of democracy and democratisation in Africa and Middle East. Information, Society and Justice Journal, *3*(2), 81-94.

[3] Committee of Economic, S. and C. R. (2020). Statement on the Covid-19 Pandemic and Economic, Social and Cultural Rights. International Human Rights Law Review, *9*(1), 135-142. https://doi.org/10.1163/22131035-00901006

[4] Kolstad, I., & Wiig, A. (2018). Diversification and democracy. International Political Science Review, *39*(4), 551-569. https://doi.org/10.1177/0192512116679833

[5] Mngomezulu, B. (2019). Assessing the suitability of the proportional representation electoral system for Southern. Journal of African Foreign Affairs, *6*(2), 157-171. https://doi.org/10.31920/2056-5658/2019/v6n2a8

[6] Oostveen, A. M., & van den Besselaar, P. (2004). Internetne glasovalne tehnologije in držvljanska participacija z vidika uporabnikov. Javnost, *11*(1), 61-78. https://doi.org/10.1080/13183222.2004.11008847

[7] Vinkel, P. (2012). Internet Voting: Experiences From Five Elections in Estonia. In *Democracy and Development—Taiwan and Baltic Countries in Comparative*.

[8] Canada-Europe Transatlantic Dialogue. (2010). *A Comparative Assessment of Electronic Voting Prepared for Elections Canada*. Retrieved from https://carleton.ca/canadaeurope/wp-content/uploads/AComparativeAssessmentofInternetVoting FINALFeb19-a-1.pdf

[9] Gilmore, J., & Howard, P. N. (2014). The internet and democracy in global perspective: Voters, candidates, parties, and social movements. In *Internet, Voting, and Democracy* (pp. 43-56). Retrieved from https://books.google.co.zw/books?id=QD65BQAAQBAJ&pg=PA8&dq=Remote+Internet+voting+is+voting+by+Internet+from+the+voter's+home+or+potentially+any+other+place+with+Internet+access&hl=en&sa=X&ved=0ahUKEwjZx9q437PlAhUvVBUIHajzCWwQ6AEIJjAA#v=onepage&q=Remote I

[10] Sambo, P. (2019). *eVoting in the SADC Region: Behavioural issues affecting its implementation in Namibia and South Africa*. University of South Africa.

[11] Chisinau. (2016). *Feasibility study on Internet Voting for the Central Electoral Commission of the Republic of Moldova*.

[12] Faulí C., Stewart K., Porcu F., Taylor J., Theben A., Baruch B., Folkvord F., Nederveen F., L.-V. F., & Devaux A. (2018). Study on the benefits and drawbacks of remote voting solutions - Presentation of Main findings.

[13] Christopher, G. (2018). DR Congo elections: Why do voters mistrust electronic voting? *BBC News*. Retrieved from https://www.bbc.com/news/world-africa-46555444

[14] Applegate, M., & Basysty, V. (2020). *Considerations on Internet Voting: An Overview for Electoral Decision-Makers*.

[15] McKeon, N. (2018). 'Getting to the root causes of migration' in West Africa–whose history, framing and agency counts? Globalizations, *15*(6),

870-885. https://doi.org/10.1080/14747731.2018.1503842

[16] OSAA/ACCORD/AU/IOM. (2015). Conflict-Induced Migration in Africa: Maximizing New Opportunities to Address its Peace, Security and Inclusive Development Dimensions. *Major Global and Continental Trends on Migration ; Impact on Affected African Migrant Populations*, (November), 23-24.

[17] Giles, C., & Mwai, P. (2021). Africa internet: Where and how are governments blocking it? *BBC News*. Retrieved from https://www.bbc.com/news/world-africa-47734843

[18] Schmidt, A., Heinson, D., Langer, L., Opitz-Talidou, Z., Richter, P., Volkamer, M., & Buchmann, J. (2009). Developing a Legal Framework for Remote Electronic Voting. In P. Ryan & B. Schoenmakers (Eds.), *Evoting and identity second international conference VOTEID 2009 Luxembourg September 78 2009 proceedings* (pp. 92-105). Springer. https://doi.org/10.1007/978-3-642-04135-8_6

[19] Corrigan, T. (2020). *Africa's ICT infrastructure: Its present and prospects*. SAIIA Policy Briefing (Vol. 197). Retrieved from https://saiia.org.za/research/africas-ict-infrastructure-its-present-and-prospects/#

[20] Sarkar, A., Pick, J. B. ., & Johnson, J. (2015). Africa's digital divide: Geography, policy, and implications. In *Regional ITS Conference, Los Angeles 146339, International Telecommunications Society (ITS)*.

[21] Epstein, J. (2010). *Internet Voting, Security, and Privacy. Bill of Rights Journal William & Mary Bill of Rights* Journal (Vol. 19). Retrieved from http://www.time.com/time/politics/article/0,8599,2025696,00.html

[22] Schryen, G. (2010). Security aspects of Internet based voting. *Department of Economical Computer Science Und Operations Research*. https://doi.org/10.1007/978-90-481-3662-9_56

[23] Rodríguez-Pérez, A., Valletbó-Montfort, P., & Cucurull, J. (2019). Bringing transparency and trust to elections: Using blockchains for the transmission and tabulation of results. In *ACM International Conference Proceeding Series* (Vol. Part F148155, pp. 46-55). New York, NY, USA: Association for Computing Machinery. https://doi.org/10.1145/3326365.3326372

[24] Sambo, P., & Alexander, P. (2018). A scheme of analysis for eVoting as a technological innovation system. Electronic Journal of Information Systems in Developing Countries, *84*(2), e12020. https://doi.org/10.1002/isd2.12020

[25] Gibb, R. (2016). Electoral violence in sub-Saharan Africa: causes and consequences. African Affairs, *115*(461), 766-767. https://doi.org/10.1093/afraf/adw061

[26] Volkamer, M., Spycher, O., & Dubuis, E. (2011). Measures to establish trust in internet voting. In *ACM International Conference Proceeding Series* (pp. 1-10). New York, New York, USA: ACM Press. https://doi.org/10.1145/2072069.2072071

[27] Trechsel, A. H. (2017). *POTENTIAL AND CHALLENGES OF E-VOTING IN THE EUROPEAN UNION STUDY*. Retrieved from http://www.europarl.europa.eu/RegData/etudes/STUD/2016/556948/IPOL_STU%282016%29556948_EN.pdf

[28] Solvak, M. (2020). Does vote verification work: Usage and impact of confidence building technology in internet voting. In *Electronic Voting - 5th International Joint Conference, E-Vote-ID 2020, Bregenz, Austria, October 6-9, 2020, Proceedings|* (Vol. 12455 LNCS, pp. 213-228). Springer Science and Business

Media Deutschland GmbH. https://doi.org/10.1007/978-3-030-60347-2_14

[29] Mueller, R. S. (2019). Report On The Investigation Into Russian Interference In The 2016 Presidential Election, *I*(March).

[30] Soni, Y., Maglaras, L., & Ferrag, M. A. (2020). Blockchain based voting systems. *European Conference on Information Warfare and Security,* ECCWS, 2020-June, 241-248. https://doi.org/10.34190/EWS.20.122

[31] Yi, O. K., & Das, D. (2020). Block chain technology for electronic voting. Journal of Critical Reviews, *7*(3), 114-124. https://doi.org/10.31838/jcr.07.03.22

[32] Africa Union. (2020). The digital transformation strategy for Africa (2020-2030).

Chapter 5

Clinical Pathway for Improving Quality Service and Cost Containtment in Hospital

Abstract

The explanation begins with the Clinical Pathway in Hospital which describes how the Clinical Pathway is used in relation to 2 things: Components-Linkages and Step-Problems-Optimal Solution, followed by Linkages Clinical Pathway with Quality Improvement and Cost Containment, which describes the relationship of each. Followed by the Clinical Pathway for Service Quality: which consists of: (1) Clinical Pathway for Service Quality, (2) Patient Safety for Service Quality Improvement, (3) The role of alogarithm, thereby clarifying the form of clinical pathways in quality improvement efforts that ensure service improvement by still maintain the quality that is maintained during the cost containment. The Clinical Pathway in Cost Containment describes the roles of: (1) Link of Components, (2) Procedure, (3) Unit Cost, so that cost containment efforts can be made in the form of cost containment optimally while maintaining quality does not need to decrease. Clinical Pathway in New Era is a newly developed algorithm related to current and future conditions. This is related to: (1) New Era in Pandemic Covid-19, (2) Clinical Pathway in Non Curative Service, (3) Clinical Pathway in Technology Services, (4) Clinical Pathway in Technological Rerelated while continuing to carry out quality improvement and cost containment simultaneously. Concluton: clinical pathway in hospital can be used as a system for Quality Improvement and Cost Containment, related to New Era in Pandemic Covid-19, Non Curative Service, Technology Services and Technological Rerelated.

Keywords: clinical pathway, quality improvement, cost containment, pandemic covid-19, non curative service, technology services, technological rerelated

1. Introduction

1.1 Clinical pathway in hospital

Clinical Pathway [1] is an effort made in order to:

1. Outlines the steps in detail:

2. Outlines the important steps that must be taken;

3. Describe services to patients;

4. Estimate possible clinical problems.

The description above provides directions to make it easier to discuss and try to get the same understanding, thus further formulation can be carried out to find clinical problems that may occur and provide directions for possible solutions, so that optimal conditions or the best conditions can be considered in existing conditions. This will be important for the following 3 things:

1. Provide an overview of the optimal service quality conditions;

2. Linkage with the best activity steps of cost-related services;

3. Clear activity as part of the steps that an algorithm can make, so that software can be made for computer or smartphone applicants.

Now with more advanced and superior computerization advancements, help simplify the complex problems of the Clinical Pathway, thus providing a discussion space for clinicians and hospital management to:

1. The use of the Clinical Pathway, its components and relationships that are clinically correct and in optimal management, an understanding that has often become difficult;

2. Provide steps, problems and optimal solutions, so that cost calculations can be carried out and rationally accepted.

The following are examples related to the role of clinical pathways in effectiveness [2]: clarity of admission, interventions, comparison of old and new therapies and clearer outcomes of clinical pathways. In this condition, the use of computerization makes it easier to explain and simulate events. The relationship of the above becomes clearer as described, as follows.

1. Components-relation to clinical pathway

Components in the right and correct clinical pathway are important, because it determines the appropriate diagnosis and is associated with appropriate clinical reasoning [3], otherwise it will be very dangerous related to misdiagnosis. The existence of various components that can be replaced or substituted is a challenge to keep choosing the right and right choice, as well as linkages that remain in the right and precise order according to Clinical Resioning while still guided by the flow of diagnosis as well as the correct therapy. Any mistake in the association will be dangerous to diagnosis and therapy, which can be dangerous for the patient. In the use of algorithms in the use of information systems in the Clinical Pathway, components and relationships play an important role in maintaining compatibility between clinical Reasioning and computational logic. The role of the fields of Information Technology, Medical and Medical Informatics is to jointly guard the condition of the components and their activities correctly and correctly.

2. Step-problem-optimal solution

Actually the best is the ideal or maximum, this is one that is intact from the world of medicine which is classified as an art, although some things have been replaced by tools and computerization. Determination of Step-Problem-Solution requires clinical reasoning, judgment, and experience so it is necessary to have an alternative companion, including still considering any possible side effects. Again, the role of Medical, Information Technology and Medical Informatics [4] or Information System experts is important to guard not only accuracy-truth, also Step-Problem-Solution, it is also necessary to consider the existence of patient safety [5].

1.2 Linkages clinical pathway with quality improvement and cost containment

The existence of Component-Linkage and Step-Problem-Solution is a necessity that needs to be considered in order to achieve an optimal Clinical Pathway, so the importance of being considered is related to things like the following.

a. Quality Improvement [6] is the existence of service conditions related to the ideal or optimal quality that can be achieved, or meets the minimum or optimal quality standard requirements, thus it must be protected from decreasing quality or achieving low quality of service.

b. Cost Containment [7] must actually consider services that remain of quality, should not decrease below the minimum standard required, so it is important that Cost Containment can be carried out while maintaining the quality that does not decline. 3. Adequacy of Quality Improvement and Cost Containment in Clinical pathway, must be pursued with repeated simulations, which will be facilitated by the use of software or smartphone applications using appropriate and supportive algorithms.

It is important to note things like the following:

(1) It is necessary to pay attention to and select the quality that can be improved, related to examination, diagnosis and therapy as well as rehabilitation, in real terms with scientific developments, technology and community development, (2) so that components and steps that lead to costs are selected, and can be carried out without reducing the quality of service, related to science and technology, as well as the substitution and new sophisticated equipment at a higher or lower cost.

Thus the selection must be carried out by means of a formal and written review, so that the success rate can be measured. Described as follows, **Figure 1.**

In computerized technology, software development [8] and mobile phone applications [9] have many sophisticated technologies and procedures, but there is still a need for close cooperation between medical, information technology, hospital

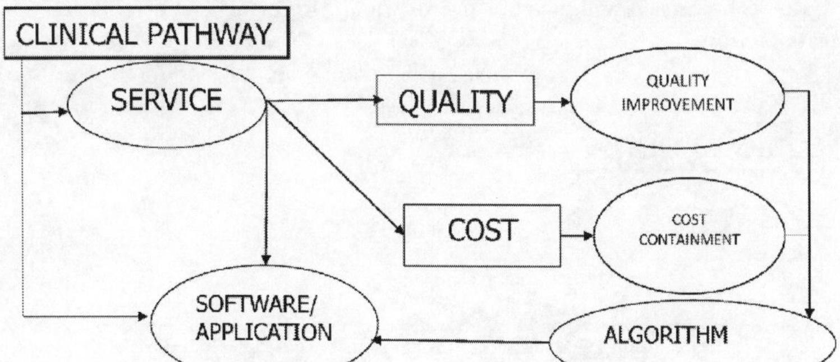

Figure 1.
Linkages clinical pathway with quality improvement and cost Cotnaimnent.

management and medical infromatics in order to manufacture form algorithm [10], so that it can be made faster and in accordance with the integrity and in harmony with the use of the application in the field with optimal results that can be achieved while still being used easily, simply and user friendly.

2. Clinical pathway for services quality improvement

2.1 Clinical pathway for service quality

The example of the Clinical Pathway algorithm for the management of malnourished patients in elderly patients, shows: clarity of steps, clarity of risk, clarity of size, clarity of time, which allows clinicians to collaborate with management; has demonstrated one quality improvement strategy [11]. Examples of the effectiveness of clinical pathways in infection disease [12], algorithms on diagnosis and therapy provide good pathways for quality improvement and also cost savings, because there are:

1. Clear and measurable steps, diagnostic steps that show a basis for the diagnosis accompanied by a measure of the likelihood of that basis;

2. Stages from beginning to end, this stage is important to develop clinical reasoning that is important in the algorithm for clinical pathways, this is important for improving service quality;

3. There are types and doses of drugs, which can be selected on the basis of the level of the type of diagnosis, in this case the therapy becomes a clear choice and can be calculated the cost burden, so at the same time cost containment efforts can be carried out.

The 3 important things above provide evidence that a Clinical Pathway can provide simultaneous direction between:

1. Quality, between components-linkages and Step-Problem-Solution, which will specifically differ for each disease diagnosis, which needs to be considered in order to maintain the quality;

2. Quality Improvement, which is the hope of the clinician, management is the patient, because it will provide improvements in the efficiency and patient satisfaction.

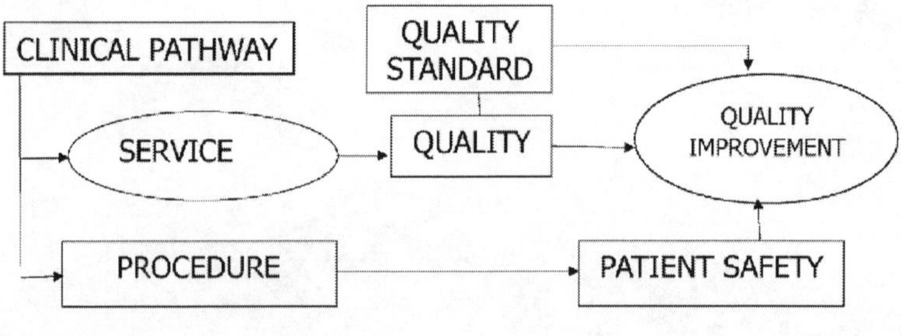

Figure 2.
Clinical pathway for quality improvement.

The relationship between Clinical Pathway and Quality Improvement [13], with its accompanying components, is illustrated as follows, **Figure 2.**

The figure above shows:

1. Related to Quality and Quality Standard [14], which will provide an overview of the extent to which must be done and especially services that meet the minimum and optimal standards;

2. Related to procedures [15] that must be carried out and the most important thing is related to patient safety, because it will allow services that save the patient, it will include simultaneously saving doctors and hospitals;

3. Prioritization in order to improve can be done simultaneously, but the fulfillment of patient safety first and then the quality standard;

4. Quality Improvement so that it is endeavored simultaneously with different levels and simultaneously achieving an optimal level.

2.2 Patient safety for service quality improvement

One of the ways of Service Quality Improvement is to use accreditation, accreditation is an effort to periodically assess the Quality Standard as the highest reference, so that our achievement is assessed against that standard. Service Quality Improvement which is important and must be a concern is Patient Safety [16], because it is one of the main goals of health services. Patient safety which is important in the hospital is the expected outcome as follows:

1. Significantly increased patient safety;

2. There is a reduction in risk and accidents;

3. There are health outcomes that are better than before;

4. There is an improved patient experience.

The four things above are related to the Quality Improvent of the service so that it will be clear what processes, outputs and outcomes will be achieved, and this effort needs to be carried out continuously and continuously, and is always a fun daily activity.

5. Optimal cost, in connection with this the existence of Cost Containment is required, it is proposed to do the following:

   a. Create a clear clinical pathway component-Linkage and Step-Problem-Optimal Solution, and can be tracked for costs;

   b. Make efforts to carry out a clear and directed Quality Improvement towards the expected quality standard;

   c. Work on Cost Containment which takes into account the quality of service, service procedures, unit costs which are simultaneously reviewed in order to create an optimal cost condition without reducing the specified quality.

2.3 Algorithm usage

The following is an example of an algorithm, which is the basis for making diagnosis and therapy, with this algorithm it can be used as a software or smartphone application. Like the following example, **Figure 3.**

The figure below shows:

1. The existence of certain steps in accordance with the direction of the signs and symptoms, in this case Heat in Adults;

2. There is a Differential Diagnosis guide;

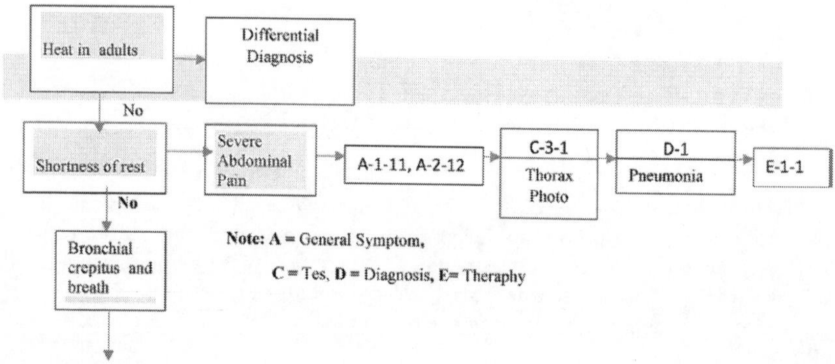

Figure 3.
Example of algorithm [17].

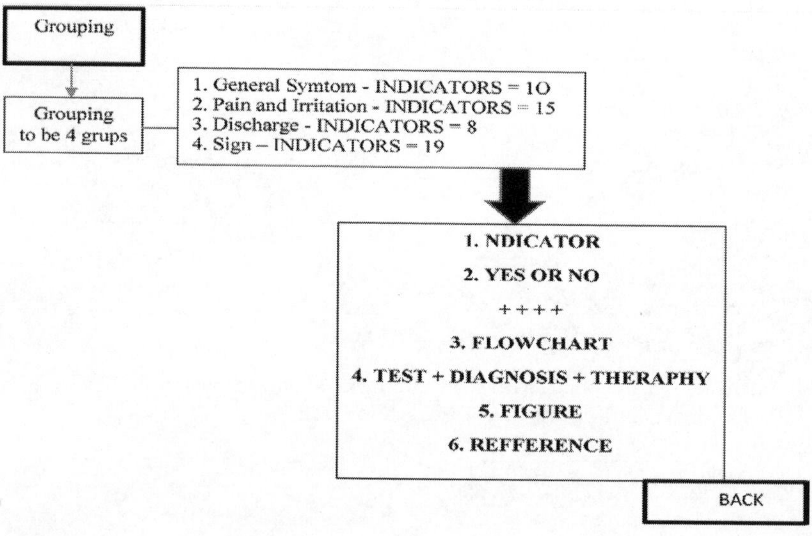

Figure 4.
Flowchart of APSIS [17].

3. There is a flow for yes and no choices;

4. If the yes path is selected it will lead to the further path-Tets-Diagnosis-Therapy.

This simple algorithm image will provide an opportunity for programmers to create software and smartphone applications, which can then be developed to examine in each of the steps which allows for quality improvement, so that it is easier to analyze shortcomings and their relationship with other steps to be improved.

Research process in the context of making APSIS (*Aplikasi Pembelajaran Alur Diagnosis dan Terapi Kedokteran* = Learning Application Flowchart of Medical Diagnosis and Therapy) in Smartphone Application, related to algorithm development can be sown as above **Figure 4.**

The figure above shows:

1. There is direction about the beginning of the start,

2. There is a division of groups which contains relatively similar indicators,

3. There are continuous steps in the form of a flowchart,

4. Provide a final description of the series, in the form of tests, diagnosis and therapy.

3. Clinical pathway in cost containment

3.1 Link of components

Cost Containment is done by maintaining the quality of service, because that is the first and important value of medical services, so the thought of costs is the next thing to consider, not the other way around. This effort can be done in terms of: [18].

1. Rates that reflect costs, with the help of Clinical Pathway and software algorithms, will easily provide remedial options, and better still provide easy possibilities for simulations by performing simulation at various costs, so that lower costs will be found while still maintain quality;

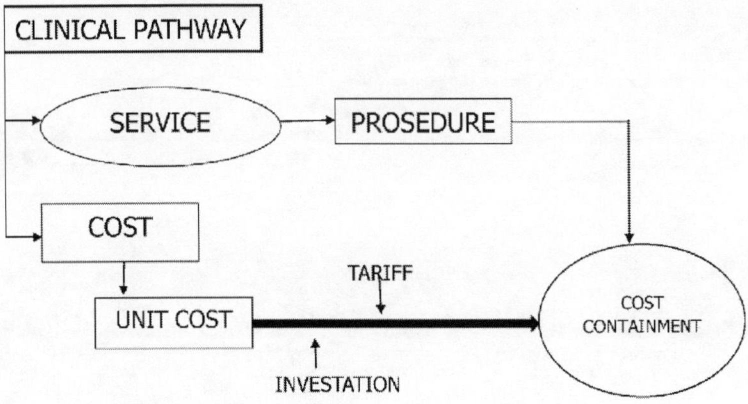

Figure 5.
Link of component in cost containment.

2. On investment, tools and instruments can now be selected which results in an easier and cheaper basis for diagnosis and therapy.

Described as follows, **Figure 5.**

3.2 Prosedure

Procedure is a series of activities that have been directed and specific in order to carry out the service, so that the service achieves the objectives as determined, in accordance with the competence of the specified executor, as **Figure 6.**

The figure below shows:

1. Procedure, will be related to equipment, material and infrastructure so as to enable services to run smoothly;

2. Related to operations, namely: time, schedule and service implementation, as well as operators to enable services to run according to their destination and time;

3. The existence of certain service specifications, which are related to available funds and determined service rates, are considered in the context of cost containment.

The 3 things above must be considered with the standard of optimal cost, and the quality of service still occurs without a decrease in quality, this is a characteristic of cost containment that is carried out properly.

3.3 Unit cost

Description related to Unit Cost [19] which is the basis for Cost Containment, related to Billing for existing Services in accordance with Quality Standards and Coding in Clinical Pathways. The figure is as below, **Figure 7.**

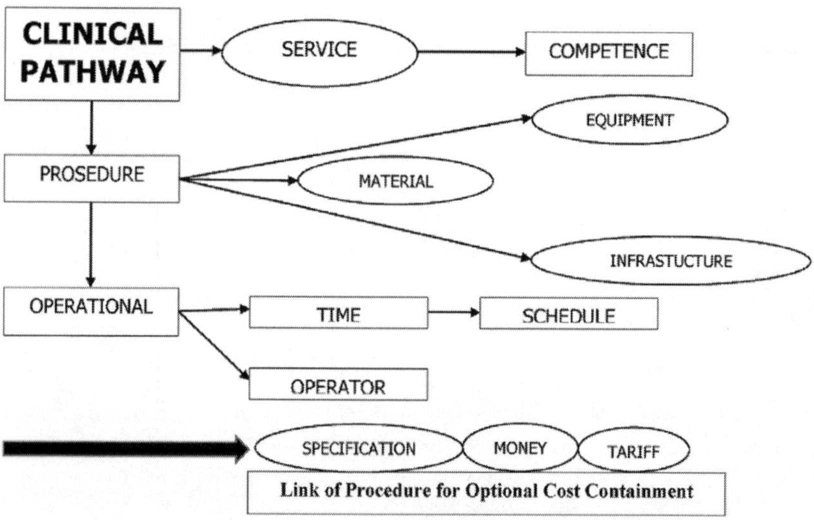

Figure 6.
Link of procedure for cost containment.

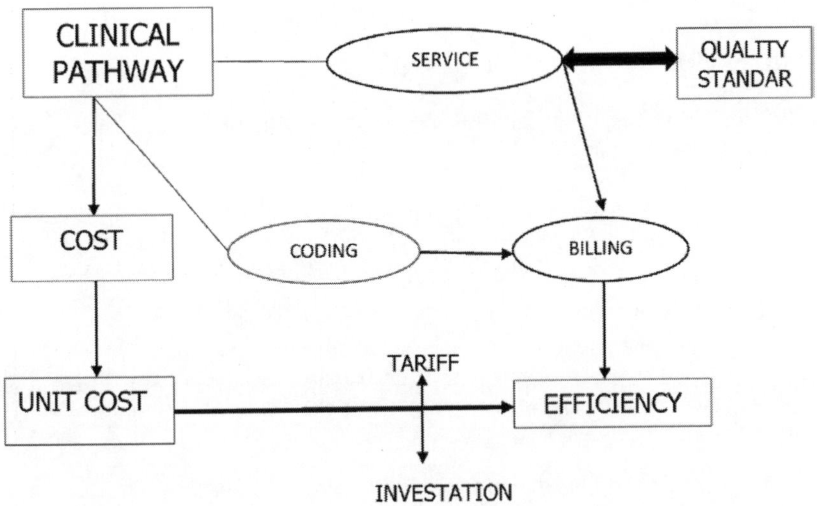

Figure 7.
Link of unit cost for cost containment.

Furthermore, the Unit Cost, as a breakdown of Cost in accordance with the required cost details, will be the basis for determining the tariff and the charging of investment, so that a complete loading will occur; thus the optimal efficiency conditions will be calculated. In this case, it will be a part that provides a limitation so that the Quality Standard does not decrease by keeping the Unit Cost from decreasing drastically which causes the Quality Standard also decline too.

4. Clinical pathway in new era

4.1 New era in pandemic Covid-19

There are 4 important things related to the Covid-19 Era Pandemic: [20]

1. Pandemic atmosphere, anxious atmosphere, lots of information circulating and often confusing, mainstay information centers are often late in reporting, so there is an atmosphere that is at least unsettled and unpleasant.

2. Daily behavior, work and trying behavior are limited and there is a health protocol, providing a new, limited atmosphere and additional rules.

3. Patients with chronic diseases, such as hypertension, diabetes, chronic lung disease and others are known as comorbid people, a label that is very susceptible to infection, so there must be special protection and treatment.

4. This is invisible to the eye, the prominent patient being treated is only limited stress [21] which can be handled alone, an iceberg phenomenon that requires special treatment which currently only focuses on physical activities. The proof is that the health protocol is very difficult to implement, it must be violent until the threat of punishment, it does not develop automatic and natural awareness.

In connection with the matters above, how is the condition of the hospital: [22]

1. Outpatient visits decreased dramatically, so admissions were reduced;

2. Additional costs for the implementation of the health protocol, required immediately and cannot be delayed,

3. Protection for medical personnel, paramedics and other personnel related to hospital services, requires extra efforts to maintain a balance of quality services with protection of health workers so that they do not become infected.

Throughout the current journey, no hospital has gone bankrupt, apart from being supported by the government with social assistance, also because the hospital can make good adjustments, or postpone the burden into the future. In this connection:

1. There is an effort to maintain quality, it remains an important task that must be carried out without adjustments that can reduce quality;

2. The existence of cost containment is an option that must be done, with all the risks and consequences, which must be done right now;

3. There is an effort to give a big role to clinical pathways and the use of computerized analysis [23] to simplify complex problems and prepare new efforts quickly and easily, in this case when normal is only an option for later, then now inevitably have to be selected and worked on now, using computerized assistance.

There are 3 important things that will immediately be used as important references in ministry in the new era, as below:

1. Clinical Pathway in Non Curative Service [24], is a service that needs attention, as part of reducing contact and cost containment, which is promoted as a service that tries to reduce curative services which are usually more expensive, which of course can only be done at certain diseases and stages of therapy only;

2. Clinical Pathway in Technology Services [25], services designed with the support of mechanical technology and information systems, thereby reducing doctor-patient contact and providing better accuracy, which may be lacking in compassionate contact;

3. Clinical Pathway in Technological Related [26], is a service that from the beginning relied on technology as a mainstay, thus the presence of doctors will be made more efficient and on matters that are important and that are not harmful.

4.2 Clinical pathway in non curative service

The application of the Clinical Pathway now and in the future requires adjustments related to earlier approaches and prevention, not just therapy, because technological advances and awareness of healthy living are being promoted. Advance clinic and treatment to an earlier direction, such as Promotive, Preventive and Rehabilitation which is more aggressive and earlier.

An example is illustrated as follows as **Figure 8.**

The current palliative approach still needs to be developed towards older and more productive patients who can still enjoy an optimal quality of life, requiring hard work and continued development.

The next explanation is as follows.

1. Promotive [27] is an effort to increase knowledge and behavior in order to have a basic knowledge in dealing with disease with 3 main activities:

a. Awareness, is an effort to make people aware, especially those who are still healthy or slightly ill, have an awareness of the dangers that lead to disease;

b. Health education, which aims to increase knowledge and society or prospective patients, or have become patients so that the prevention is more severe;

c. Education, is an effort to encourage the community or patients to improve their abilities that previously could not be, bad behavior becomes good;

d. Consulting, is an effort to help the community or patients to be able to solve existing problems, and together find solutions.

This condition is often mixed up so that efforts do not produce optimal results, the best way to suggest is to select the required picture, then adjust the handling according to need.

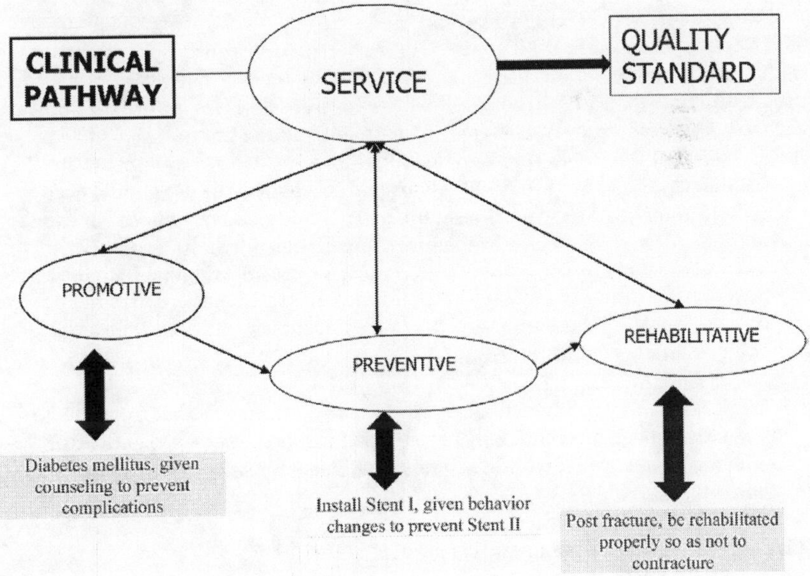

Figure 8.
Clinical pathway in non curative service.

2. Preventive [28] is an effort to prevent the disease from occurring, not getting worse, not getting worse, a common example is the use of immunization. This effort will be calculated the value of the cost that is cheaper when compared to treatment.

3. Rehabilitation [29] is an effort to make improvements to a condition that is already damaged or there is already an abnormality, so that as much as possible it can be restored as before. The current rehabilitation, many use tools and some are computerized, what is needed is a careful study so that it is sorted according to needs and the use of cost containment can be done.

4.3 Clinical pathway in technology services

The era of Telemedicine [30], with the Covid-19 Pandemic, the need to maintain distance makes it imperative to use more massive telemedicine, it is necessary to develop algorithms that are in accordance with the following: (1) there is a standard procedure and still meets clinical reasoning, (2) services that can be carried out gradually Quality Improvement, (3) services that can be simultaneously carried out cost Contaiment optimally but reduce quality. This presents a challenge, not only for doctors, hospitals, Information Communication Technology and Medical Informatics experts, to collectively achieve the above expectations.

The robotic era [31] will be greatly stimulated by the Covid-19 Pandemic by trying to avoid contact between doctors and patients in order to prevent transmission. The differences that occur are: (1) the procedure will be relatively the same, dealing with the patient is a robot, (2) the doctor controls the robot, not the instrument, also the time and sequence will be clear and can be calculated. Increasingly sophisticated computer performance with large capacities, supported by Artificial Intelligent, provides challenges, and at the same time, care must be taken with regard to patient safety, not according to good tools, still violating the patient safety principle.

The era of the Internet of Things [32] is a challenge now in various countries with a large number of elderly people, several countries have happened, some countries are not less than 10 years old will be a heavy burden. Thus the use of: Clinical Pathway, Quality Improvement, Cost Contaiment and the Internet of Things will be the way out that is needed. An example illustration is as follows as **Figure 9.**

The description above provides options and accelerates the use of advanced technology and with large capacities more quickly and relatively forced, due to the Covid-19 Pandemic which requires maintaining distance, avoiding contact and avoiding relatively long trips. Anticipation must be developed immediately with the following standards:

1. Keep following Clinical Reasoning and Clinical Pathway which are based on service quality standards;

2. Developing Quality Improvement and Cost Containment that are relevant and balanced, so that the perspective is accepted by doctors, hospitals, patients and insurers.

4.4 Clinical pathway in technological related

1. Heath Electronic Record (HER) or Medical Record (MR) [33] related to electronic medical records, which is getting more and more advanced with regard to voice recognition which provides direct recording of the history, and video

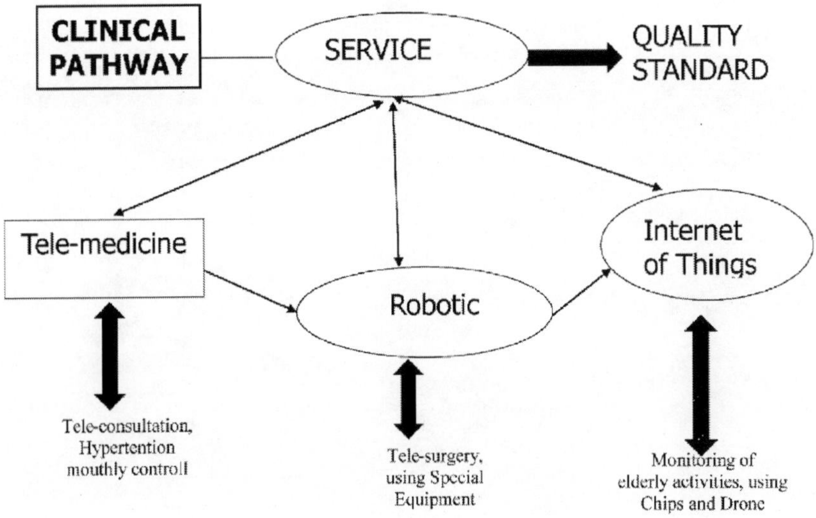

Figure 9.
Clinical pathway in technology services.

recognition which records examination conditions using video in an integrated manner. The importance of an integrated and electronically based Medical Record (MR) provides:

a. Higher speed;

b. Clearer accuracy, greater capacity and high access, also with completeness, will help Quality Improvement;

c. Conditions that will impose large costs, which require Cost Containment to achieve optimal efficiency and cost load; with the Direct Consultation tool, the patient can consult a doctor or a robot, for several diseases that have been standardized first.

d. Tele-device [34], is a device that can be controlled remotely, or performs remote inspection, so that examinations that use certain tools do not need people to come from a distant city, just at the initial place, the results of the examination can be sent including the description. This is important for reference and preparedness in the context of Covid-19.

e. Self Service [35] with a standardized algorithm, a Guidance Commission Support System can be used to make diagnosis and therapy of diseases. In this case, Quality Improvement and Cost Containment is important in giving choices, because the decision is made by the patient, it may need to be limited to chronic disease and regular control and options that are not feasible.

2. A simple example illustration as follows as **Figure 10.**

The above description is broader as below.

1. Consultations, with real doctors, with robots that use voice or video can be carried out, which requires an unbeatable Clinical Pathway Algorithm, so the

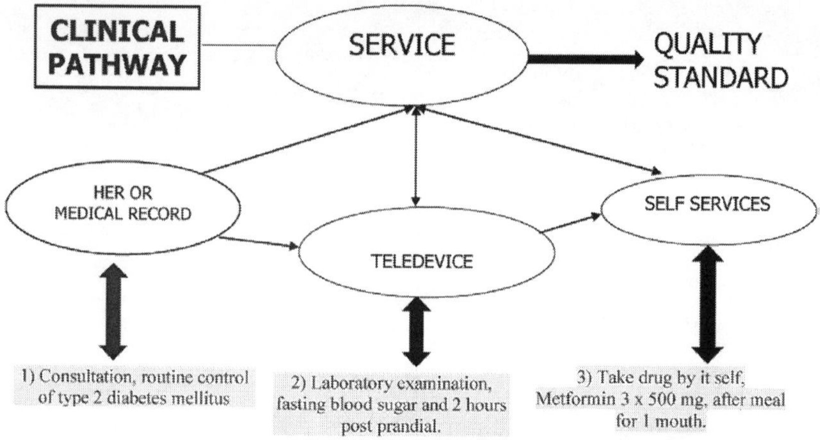

Figure 10.
Clinical pathway in technological related.

Quality Improvement role is very important and must be made from the time the services and software are used.

2. Examinations such as laboratories, methods, reagents and result criteria must be clear about the normal and maximum or minimum standards that apply, this is related to so that patients do not need to think a lot and do not need to learn clinical reasoning, but precisely in a safe corridor. This Cost Containment becomes important, especially in choosing a relatively cheap and safe examination.

3. Self-medicating, determining the usual diagnosis and therapy and in a safe category, can be done as long as it is normally done, without complications and there are new diagnoses and therapies. Quality Improvement and Cost Containment simultaneously to ensure high quality at optimal cost.

5. Conclution

Clinical pathway in hospital is an effort made in order to: outlines the steps in detail, outlines the important steps that must be taken, describe services to patients and estimate possible clinical problems; it can be used as a system for Quality Improvement and Cost Containment. The effectiveness of clinical pathways in algorithms on diagnosis and therapy provide good pathways for quality improvement and also cost savings. Cost Containment is done by maintaining the quality of service, because that is the first and important value of medical services, so the thought of costs is the next thing to consider, not the other way around. The Cost Containment effort can be done in terms of rates that reflect costs, with the help of Clinical Pathway that lower costs will be found while still maintain quality. Clinical Pathway that is used on investment, tools and instruments can now be selected which results cheaper basis for diagnosis and therapy. There are important things that will immediately be used as references in the new era that related to New Era in Pandemic Covid-19, Non Curative Service, Technology Services and Technological Rerelated, biside that Clinical Pathway will be made more efficient and on matters that are important and that are not harmful.

References

[1] Kinsman, L, at. al, *What is a clinical pathway? Development of a definition to inform the debate,* May 2010, BMC Medicine 8(1):31, DOI: 10.1186/1741-7015-8-31, PubMed, https://www.researchgate.net/publication/44635168_What_is_a_clinical_pathway_Development_of_a_definition_to_inform_the_debate/link/0912f5058dc7af283f000000/download, 2020-09-26, 9:21 PM

[2] Iroth1,R.A.M., Achadi, A., *The Impact of Clinical Pathway to Effectiveness of Patient Care In Current Medical Practice In Hospital:A Literature Review*, Proceedings of International Conference on Applied Science and Health (No. 4, 2019), ICHSH-A111, https://publications.inschool.id/index.php/icash/article/view/432/344, 2020-09-9:26 PM

[3] Michele Groves, Peter O'Rourke, Heather Gwendoline, & Innes Alexander, *The clinical reasoning characteristics of diagnostic experts*, June 2003, Medical Teacher 25(3):308-13, DOI: 10.1080/0142159031000100427, Source PubMed, download: https://www.researchgate.net/publication/10644625_The_clinical_reasoning_characteristics_of_diagnostic_experts, 2020-11-24, 10:40 PM

[4] Emma Aspland, Daniel Gartner & Paul Harper, *Clinical pathway modelling: a literature review*, September 2019, Health Systems, DOI: 10.1080/20476965.2019.1652547, License CC BY 4.0, download: https://www.researchgate.net/publication/335764923_Clinical_pathway_modelling_a_literature_review, 2020-11-24, 10:50 PM

[5] Danielsson, Marita; Nilsen, Per; Rutberg, Hans; Årestedt, Kristofer, *A National Study of Patient Safety Culture in Hospitals in Sweden,* Journal of Patient Safety: December 2019 - Volume 15 - Issue 4 - p 328-333 doi: 10.1097/PTS.0000000000000369, download: https://journals.lww.com/journalpatientsafety/Fulltext/2019/12000/A_National_Study_of_Patient_Safety_Culture_in.18.aspx?WT.mc_id=HPxADx20100319xMP, 2020-11-23, 11:15PM

[6] Adam Backhouse quality improvement programme lead & Fatai Ogunlayi public health specialty registrar, *Quality improvement into practice*, BMJ 2020;368:m865 doi: 10.1136/bmj.m865 (Published 31 March 2020), download: https://www.bmj.com/content/bmj/368/bmj.m865.full.pdfhttps://www.bmj.com/content/bmj/368/bmj.m865.full.pdf, 2020-11-24, 10;23

[7] Niek Stadhouders, Florien Krusea, Marit Tankea, Xander Koolmanb, Patrick Jeurissena,c Niek Stadhouders, Florien Krusea, Marit Tankea, Xander Koolmanb, Patrick Jeurissena, *Effective healthcare cost-containment policies: A systematic review*, 2018 The Authors. Published by Elsevier Ireland Ltd. This is an open access article under the CC BY-NC-ND license (http://creativecommons.org/licenses/by-nc-nd/4.0/), download: https://academie-nieuwezorg.nl/wp-content/uploads/2019/04/Patrick-Jeurissen-Effective-healthcare-cost-containment-policies-A-systematic-review.pdf, 2020-11-24, 11:23 PM

[8] **M F** Aarnoutse, Sjaak Brinkkemper, Marleen de Mul & Marjan Askari, *Pros and Cons of Clinical Pathway Software Management: A Qualitative Study*, January 2018, Studies in health technology and informatics 247:526-530, download: https://www.researchgate.net/publication/324686817_Pros_and_Cons_of_Clinical_Pathway_Software_Management_A_Qualitative_Study, 2020-11-27, 9:55

[9] Aida Aalrazek, *Effect of Implementing Clinical Pathway to Improve Child-Birth and Neonatal Outcomes*, October 2018, American Journal of Nursing Research 6(6):454-465, DOI: 10.12691/ajnr-6-6-13, download: https://www.researchgate.net/publication/328742132_Effect_of_Implementing_Clinical_Pathway_to_Improve_Child-Birth_and_Neonatal_Outcomes, 2020-11-27, 10:42

[10] Emma Aspland, Daniel Gartner & Paul Harp, *Clinical pathway modelling: a literature review*, September 2019, Health Systems, DOI: 10.1080/20476965.2019.1652547, License CC BY 4.0, download: https://www.researchgate.net/publication/335764923_Clinical_pathway_modelling_a_literature_reviewhttps://www.researchgate.net/publication/335764923_Clinical_pathway_modelling_a_literature_review.

[11] Thomas Rotter, Robert Baatenburg de Jong, Sara Evans Lacko, Ulrich Ronellenfitsch, and Leigh Kinsman, *Improving healthcare quality in Europe: Characteristics, effectiveness and implementation of different strategies [Internet]*, https://www.ncbi.nlm.nih.gov/books/NBK549262/, 2020-09-26, 9:36 PM

[12] Bahar Madrana, Şiran Keskeb, Soner Uzunc, Tolga Taymazc, Emine Bakırc,_ Ismail Bozkurtd, Önder Ergönüle, *Effectiveness of clinical pathway for upper respiratory tractinfections in emergency department*, international Journal of Infectious Diseases 83 (2019) 154-159, https://pubmed.ncbi.nlm.nih.gov/31051280/, 2020-10-02, 11:59 PM

[13] Leigh Kinsman, *Clinical pathway compliance and quality improvement*, January 2004, Nursing standard: official newspaper of the Royal College of Nursing 18(18):33-5, DOI: 10.7748/ns.18.18.33.s51, Source PubMed, download: https://www.researchgate.net/publication/8882049_Clinical_pathway_compliance_and_quality_improvement, 2020-11-27, 11:02

[14] American Diabetes Association, *American Diabetes Association Standards of Medical Care in Diabetesd2019*, Diabetes Care Volume 42, Supplement 1, January 2019, download: https://care.diabetesjournals.org/content/diacare/suppl/2018/12/17/42.Supplement_1.DC1/DC_42_S1_2019_UPDATED.pdf, 2020-11-27, 11:16

[15] Elaine Mormer and Joel Stevans, *Clinical Quality Improvement and Quality Improvement Research*, https://doi.org/10.1044/2018_PERS-ST-2018-0003, download: https://pubs.asha.org/doi/full/10.1044/2018_PERS-ST-2018-0003, 2020-11-28, 3:04 PM

[16] WHO, *Patient Safety Making health care* , download: https://apps.who.int/iris/bitstream/handle/10665/255507/WHO-HIS-SDS-2017.11-eng.pdf, 2020-11-23, 11:38 PM

[17] Sabarguna, B.S, *APSIS*, https://play.google.com/store/apps/details?id=com.apsismvt.android, 2020-11-20, 1:48

[18] Romeyke, T & Stummer, H., *Clinical Pathways as Instruments for Risk and Cost Management in Hospitals - A Discussion Paper*, Global Journal of Health Science, ol. 4, No. 2; March 2012, doi:10.5539/gjhs.v4n2p50, https://www.ncbi.nlm.nih.gov/pmc/articles/PMC4777053/pdf/GJHS-4-50.pdf, 2020-10-03: 12:59 AM

[19] NiekStadhouders, FlorienKruse, MaritTanke, XanderKoolman, PatrickJeurissen, *Effective healthcare cost-containment policies: A systematic review*, Health Policy, Volume 123, Issue 1, January 2019, Pages 71-79, https://doi.org/10.1016/j.healthpol.2018.10.015, download: https://www.sciencedirect.com/science/article/pii/S0168851018306341, 2020-11-28, 4:04 PM

[20] Budi Yanti , Eko Mulyadi, Wahiduddin, Revi Gama Hatta Novika, Yuliana Mahdiyah Da'at Arina, Natalia Sri Martani, & Nawan, *Knowledge, Attitudes, and Behavior Towards Social Distancing Policy as A Means Community of Preventing Transmission of Covid-19 in Indonesia*, Jurnal Administrasi Kesehatan Indonesia Vol 8 No 1 Special Issue 2020 Published by Universitas Airlangga Doi: 10.20473/jaki.v8i2.2020.4-14, download: https://journals.sagepub.com/doi/full/10.1177/0022034520914246, 2020-11-28, 9;41 PM

[21] WHO, *Doing What Matters in Times of Stress,* download: https://www.who.int/publications/i/item/9789240003927?gclid=Cj0KCQiAh4j-BRCsARIsAGeV12D5JjhAG8uXXbsH0xYIxfUDYKLXs9DXoM1Nq-ONJaT-rr34OAc97xgaAgLBEALw_wcB, 2020-11-28, 9:54 PM

[22] John D. Birkmeyer, Amber Barnato, Nancy Birkmeyer, Robert Bessler & Jonathan Skinner, *Impact Of The COVID-19 Pandemic On Hospital Admissions The In The United States,* Health Afair, September 2020, download: https://www.healthaffairs.org/doi/pdf/10.1377/hlthaff.2020.00980, 2020-11-28, 10:06

[23] Raju Vaishya, Abid Haleem, Abhishek Vaish & Mohd Javaid, *Emerging technologies to combat COVID-19 pandemic*, May 2020, Journal of Clinical and Experimental Hepatology 10(4), DOI: 10.1016/j.jceh.2020.04.019, download: https://www.researchgate.net/publication/341167896_Emerging_technologies_to_combat_COVID-19_pandemic, 2020-11-28, 10:17.

[24] Liezl Balfour, Isabel Coetzee & Tanya Heyns, *Developing a clinical pathway for non-invasive ventilation*, December 2012, International Journal of Care Pathways 16(4):107-114, DOI: 10.1258/jicp.2012.012011, Project: UP - Community of Practice project, download: https://www.researchgate.net/publication/258140243_Developing_a_clinical_pathway_for_non-invasive_ventilation, 2020-11-10;30 PM

[25] Jungeun Lim , Kidong Kim , Minsu Cho , Hyunyoung Baek , Seok Kim , Hee Hwang , Sooyoung Yoo , & Minseok Song, *Deriving a sophisticated clinical pathway based on patient conditions from electronic health record data,* https://pods4h.com/wp-content/uploads/2020/10/PODS4H_2020_paper_14.pdf, 2020-11-29, 1:52

[26] Graham P. Martin, David Kocman, Timothy Stephens, Carol J. Peden &Rupert M. Pears, *Pathways to professionalism? Quality improvement, care pathways, and the interplay of standardisation and clinical autonomy*, Firest published: 21 June 2017, Sociology of Health & Illness Vol. 39 No. 8 2017 ISSN 0141-9889, pp. 1314-1329 Sociology of Health & Illness Vol. 39 No. 8 2017 ISSN 0141-9889, pp. 1314-1329, Doi: 10.1111/1467-9566.12585, download: https://onlinelibrary.wiley.com/doi/10.1111/1467-9566.12585, 2020-11-29,1:59 PM

[27] WHO, Editor: Oliver Groene & Mila Garcia-Barbero, *Health promotion in hospitals: Evidence and quality management,* Country Systems, Policies and Services Division of Country Support WHO Regional Office for Europe, May 2005, download: https://www.euro.who.int/__data/assets/pdf_file/0008/99827/E86220.pdf, 2020-11-29, 3:34 PM

[28] Nathan R. Every, Judith Hochman, Richard Becker, Steve Kopecky, Christopher P. Cannon, *the Committee on Acute Cardiac Care*, Council on Clinical Cardiology, American Heart Association, Originally published 1 Feb 2000, doi: 10.1161/01.CIR.101.4.461, Circulation. 2000;101:461-465, download: https://www.ahajournals.org/doi/full/10.1161/01.cir.101.4.461, 2020-11-29, 3:44 PM

[29] P. Rouanet, A. Mermoud, M. Jarlier, N. Bouazza, A. Laine, H. Mathieu Daudé, *Combined robotic approach and enhanced recovery after surgery pathway for optimization of costs in patients undergoing proctectomy,* First published: 30 April 2020, doi:10.1002/bjs5.50281, download: https://bjssjournals.onlinelibrary.wiley.com/doi/full/10.1002/bjs5.50281, 2020-11-29, 3:54 PM

[30] Maria Victoria Concepcion P. Cruz, Policarpio B. Joves, Jr., Noel L. Espallardo, Anna Guia O. Limpoco, Jane Eflyn Lardizabal-Bunyi, Nenacia Ranali Nirena P. Mendoza, Michael Ian N. Sta. Maria, Jake Bryan S. Cortez, Mark Joseph D. Bitong, Johann Iraj H. Montemayor, *Clinical Pathway for the Diagnosis and Management of Patients with COVID-19 in Family Practice*, download: http://thepafp.org/website/wp-content/uploads/2018/09/PAFP-Clinical-Pathway-for-the-Diagnosis-and-Management-of-Patients-with-COVID-19-in-Family-Practice.pdf, 2020-11-29, 2:33 PM

[31] Zrinjka DOLIC, Rosa CASTRO & Andrei MOARCAS, IN-DEPTH ANALYSIS Requested by the ENVI committee, *Robots in healthcare: a solution or a problem?,* Policy Department for Economic, Scientific and Quality of Life Policies Directorate-General for Internal Policies Authors: Zrinjka DOLIC, Rosa CASTRO, Andrei MOARCAS PE 638.391 - April 2019, download: https://www.europarl.europa.eu/RegData/etudes/IDAN/2019/638391/IPOL_IDA(2019)638391_EN.pdf, 2020-11-29, 2:48 PM

[32] Vijayakannan Sermakani, *Transforming healthcare through Internet of Things*, Robert Bosch Engineering and Business Ltd, download: https://pmibangalorechapter.in/pmpc/2014/tech_papers/healthcare.pdf, 2020-11-29, 2:56 PM

[33] Yiye Zhang, Rema Padman & Larry Wasserman, Show all 6 authors, Qizhi Xie, *On Clinical Pathway Discovery from Electronic Health Record Data*, January 2015, Intelligent Systems, IEEE 30(1):70-75, DOI: 10.1109/MIS.2015.14, download: https://www.researchgate.net/publication/272398045_On_Clinical_Pathway_Discovery_from_Electronic_Health_Record_Data, 2020-11-29, 3:12 PM

[34] Abayomi Salawu, Angela Green, Michael G. Crooks, Nina Brixey, Denise H. Ross, and Manoj Sivan, *A Proposal for Multidisciplinary Tele-Rehabilitation in the Assessment and Rehabilitation of COVID-19 Survivors,* International Journal of Environmental Research and Public HealthDownload: https://www.mdpi.com/1660-4601/17/13/4890/pdf, 2020-11-29, 3:19 PM

[35] Marc Gutenstein, John W Pickering & Martin Than, *Development of a digital clinical pathway for emergency medicine: Lessons from usability testing and implementation failure,* Helath Infromatics Journal, First Published June 15, 2018, Research Article, Find in PubMed, doi: 10.1177/1460458218779099, download: https://journals.sagepub.com/doi/full/10.1177/1460458218779099, 2020-11-29, 2:27 PM

Chapter 6

Interdisciplinary Integrated Tools to Problem Solving 2.0

Abstract

Everyone understands the events they witness or read about according to their mental models, and that is one of the main reasons there are a lot of disagreements at workplaces and between friends and families. Considering this situation, plus the difficulty that most people face when trying to conceptualize problems, I suggest a course that includes series methodologies, working synergistically to deal with this problem that goes from understanding the differences between people to test multiple hypotheses and planning the solution implementation. Since 2014, I have been teaching with some colleagues this tool in the format of a short course that articulates systems thinking, mapping studies, information quality, and competing hypotheses. This course has been presented often not only in Argentina and also in Peru with great success. Considering the pandemic situation, since 2020, it has been taught virtually. The latest modification to the original structure of the course was the incorporation of the Gantt chart to design the implementation of the solution found. This paper will present our course and the logic behind it, its outcomes, and how it evolved with the different iterations.

Keywords: problem-solving, systemic thinking, information quality, decision making

1. Introduction

Being part of the information society and live in this time has a lot of advantages but pose a lot of challenges. The superabundance of information and the difficulties we face to evaluate its quality complicates our decision-making processes.

The COVID-19 pandemic has shown us clearly the impact of misinformation and how the constant influx of a lot of information -of which we know just little-affects our emotional and physical health and our understanding of reality and its evolution.

Since we are running like headless chickens most of the time after many objectives that become difficult to identify, when it comes the moment to think and conceptualize a problem, we need extra help to do it properly and get the expected result. This situation also affects how we look for information and based on which parameters we select it or not, how we validate our hypothesis, and how we plan what we need to do to implement the desired solution.

Here, I will describe the course and the different methodologies included in it and show how they articulate to give the students an easy way to understand and solve their problems.

2. Related research

There are several problem-solving methods, nevertheless, almost all of them follow this logic (**Figure 1**). But only a few of them include methodologies to implement the different steps in a structured and auditable way. Also, in most of the cases, the people involved in the problems are not considered as no not only as possible sources of solutions but as the ones who know the most about the situation and, at the end, the ones who will be involved in the change.

Methodologies as the TRIZ/USIT [2], Six Sigma [3], the VSM (Viable Systems Model) [4] and the many problem-solving in 4 steps or 6 steps that exists in the literature offer different tactics to approach the problems and find a solution [5]. Even when they are helpful in many specific fields, they are not do not look for a fluid tool, easy to implement in all possible problems as the one presented here.

The Six Step Problem Solving Model [6], developed at the University of Arkansas at Pine Bluff, is worth to highlight because of its characteristics and reasoning close to the one that laid behind I designed. This method includes for each step one or more tools and considers the participation of the people involved.

In closing, even though many problem-solving methodologies exist, the one presented in this paper could be consider as a combination of the best of others that exist with a twist of innovation.

3. The course

This problem-solving course entails integrating five methodologies: systems theory, mapping studies, data quality, and competing hypothesis, plus the Gantt chart. Together, they allow us to go from the problem conceptualization to the hypothesis testing and plan the solution in a methodologically consistent, unbiased, and structured way.

Using a combination of methodologies in an articulated way has its origin in a request made by the Peruvian Air Force. They wanted to have a dedicated course on research methodologies. After that, the course has been successfully presented in many places. Finally, the INAP (National Institute for the Public Administration, Argentina) requested an upgrade to include implementing the solution found, and the Gantt chart was included. So now the course goes from problem identification to solution implementation.

This course starts with a discussion about mental models and how their impact in the understanding of the reality. In this specific context, helps to realize why we all disagree about problems or circumstance and facilitate the communication and agreements [7].

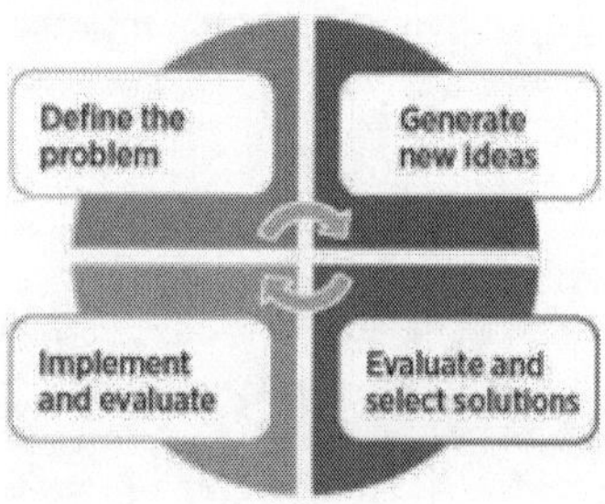

Figure 1.
Problem-solving logic [1].

3.1 General systems theory

This problem-solving course starts with understanding the first out of the five methods that conform to this proposal, the systemic method, developed after the general systems theory. This tool is well known and widely used in many disciplines.

Ludwig Von Bertalanffy, the biologist who developed the general systems theory, recognized that his theory started to be developed back in Aristotle times when he said: "the whole is greater than the sum of its parts", describing the synergy, one of the core characteristics of the system when working [8].

Von Bertalanffy included the three premises that set the basis of the General Systems Theory in his book published in 1969 [9]. Those assumptions are:

1. Systems exist within systems;

2. The systems are open; and

3. The functions of a system depend on its structure.

Von Bertalanffy has described the systems' functioning considering the inputs, processes and components and output (**Figure 2**).

In the representation of how the systems work, it is implicit a time spam since the input enters into the system, then a process takes place, and finally the product of the process exits the system as output. Therefore, applying this method to understand a problem or situation provides us with a dynamic vision of reality, including its components.

One of the most intuitive examples of a system is the ecosystem. The word itself results from the merge of eco (house) and system. According to the Encyclopaedia Britannica, a definition of the term is: "Ecosystem, the complex of living organisms, their physical environment, and all their interrelationships in a particular unit of space" [10].

A graphic representation of the ecosystem definition using systems theory could be (**Figure 3**):

The components of an ecosystem are related so a balance between them is achieved. This is another property of the systems, and it is called homeostasis.

Feedback is one of the essential properties of the systems and what means is that the system's output re-enters again as an input. This cyclic process is also linked with the homeostasis.

Let us analyze the feedback in other system, for example in a workplace where a modification is included. One role it will play will be informing if the changes have a positive or a negative impact.

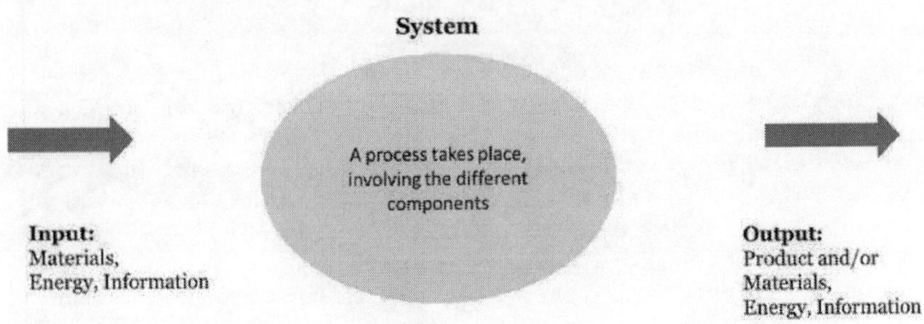

Figure 2.
How the system works (designed by the author).

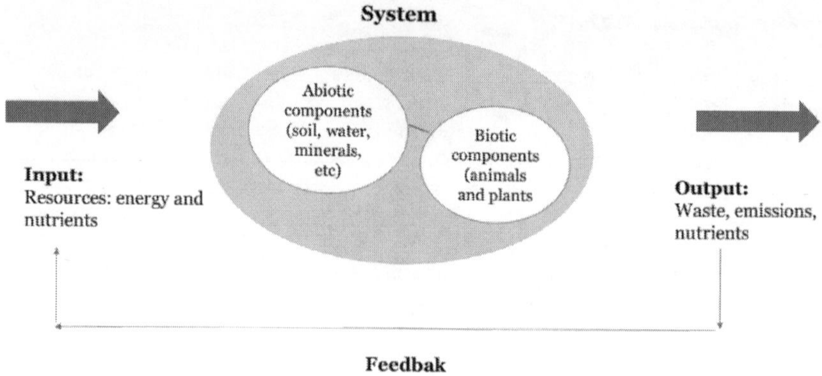

Figure 3.
Representation of an ecosystem using the systems theory (designed by the author).

The study of the systems has two possible approaches, one is the study of the system and its components and the processes that take place between them; and another is considering the border of the system, characterizing and studying what happens there. But in both cases the context is considered and the inputs and outputs (and feedback).

During the course, since this is the starting point, this method is used to conceptualize the problem and understand its components, the process, and its dynamic.

At this point, the students decide with which problem or situation they want to analyze and solve. By doing this, they move out from thinking to drafting and putting in words their ideas. This process takes time and requires reflection, and also decisions should be made to set up the limits (system border) and the components -and relations between them- of the problem under study.

When doing this conceptualization process, the system is developed with a specific objective and if the objective changes, the system will also do.

3.2 Structured searches

Once the problem is identified and described the look for answers and solutions start. At this point two possibilities exists: look for an existing solution or innovate if nothing has been done successfully by others. In both cases the search of the information in a structured way is optimal.

Considering the abundance of information, it is relevant to search on the internet following specific parameters and minimize the impact of our cognitive bias.

Systematic literature review or systematic mapping studies is the name of a methodology to execute searches in a structured way by following a detailed procedure.

The origins of this technique can be traced back to the problems the clinicians faced when relying in the available literature for their decision-making process. "In answer to this challenge, the worldwide Cochrane Collaboration was formed in 1992 to provide an expanding resource of updateable systematic reviews of randomized controlled trials (RCTs) relating to health care. Thus began the modern incarnation of the review article, a tool that had for many centuries been the mainstay for updating scientific knowledge" [11].

Later, this methodology was discovered and widely implemented by academics from the areas of systems engineering and informatics mostly to develop the state of the art of research topics. And later, considering its usefulness, it was adopted by other sciences and also used in projects design.

The author who is a reference for this methodology is Barbara Kitchencham [12] from Keele University. And Dr. Marcela Genero Bocco from the Alarcos Group (University of Castilla La Mancha -UCLM- Spain) is leading the field in Spanish-speaking countries [13].

This method is relevant in this problem-solving tool because it helps to minimize the impact of our cognitive bias when doing a search, particularly for selecting among the results. As humans, we have the tendency to tend to choose what agrees with our mental models or the concept or ideas we have in mind. Because of this, we may avoid reading relevant articles with a different perspective on the topic under study.

The methodology includes three phases: planning the review, executing it and writing the report.

In the first phase, many tasks will take place. First, the need for a review must be identified, particularly considering that applying this methodology takes time and effort and it is not for a simple quick search. By doing a review, it is possible to summarize all the information on a topic, in a format that resembles a database.

To begin with the practical steps of this tool, the research questions formulation is the next step. These research questions will be the tool to select the publications, considering whether they answer or not to them, and not how they do (this is important for the later analysis of the results). This way of selecting the publications helps to minimize the impact of our cognitive bias, allowing us to have the whole set of possible answers, and not only the ones we like.

Before performing the search, a protocol must be developed. This plan includes:

a. with what? Identification of the search terms, and also their synonyms and other alternative terms (the use OR and AND, or other Boolean operators is recommended);

b. where will the search be performed? The sources of information must be chosen and specified (use virtual libraries, Google or other search engines);

c. inclusion and exclusion criteria; and

d. a form to transfer the selected publications and the research questions must be designed, usually an Excel sheet.

In the second phase, the review takes place, and what was planned on the first phase here it is executed.

Once the search engine is selected, the terms are introduced, and the results appear. Now, it is important to check all the results, one by one, and the publications that answer the research questions will be transferred to the Excel file and the different fields will be completed. The inclusion and exclusion criteria will help to filter the results obtained, and finally the result will be a set of publications that fulfill the requirements and answer the research questions.

This methodology was designed to be implemented on virtual libraries. But it works perfectly in Google and other search engines like it.

After doing the search and filling the Excel, it will be possible to identify if an adjustment of the protocol is needed or not (new keywords, rephrase of the research questions, etc).

The publications database we will have as a result will include fields specific to each publication (author, date, publisher, title, etc.), and other relevant information, considered metadata, which will help perform a broader analysis.

The methodology concludes with the report writing. The text must include a detailed presentation of the protocol, an explanation of how the search was executed, and all the decisions made during the process to make the search repeatable and auditable.

The report will also include the analysis of the answers to the research questions, not only in writing but graphs could be performed considering the information will be included in an Excel.

This file will be the starting point to the execution of these methodologies, information quality (to evaluate the quality of the selected publications) and competing hypothesis (to identify the scenario with more support in the available literature).

3.3 Information quality core concepts

Having the possibility to access many sources of information when looking for something is fantastic. Still, the growing amount of data and information and the difficulties in knowing its quality created the need to develop a specific method to evaluate its properties [14].

Experts at the Massachusetts Institute of Technology (MIT) (Cambridge, Massachusetts, USA) developed an information quality method. Lately, professionals from other universities and countries expanded and added more elements to it.

The part of the method which will used in this problem-solving methodology is the one of categories and dimensions. The other two, that explore the role of the different stakeholders involved in the information management and the total data quality management (TDQM) cycle will not be considered here.

Wang and Strong [15], back in 1996 developed a framework to evaluate and hierarchically organize information. To create this method, they sent a survey to information consumers and master's in business administration (MBA) students asking about the most critical attributes that information should have. The result was a list of 179 attributes. After that, they performed a second survey to learn and understand the importance of the attributes identified. Finally, they come out with a list of 15 dimensions, grouped into four categories (see **Table 1**).

As the next step on the problem-solving methodology, the selected dimensions (not all are relevant in every circumstance) will be placed in Excel (from the structured search) as columns after the publication's details. A quantitative evaluation of each publication will be performed, getting at the end a value that entails the document's quality. Having these results will make it possible to rank the publications hierarchically.

3.4 Competing hypothesis

The competing hypothesis methodology was developed by Richards J. Heuer Jr., an intelligence analysis expert from the Central Intelligence Agency (CIA), during the Cold War, and a few years later was provided to the public [16].

This tool is especially useful in cases of complex problems, with many possible scenarios and a lot of evidence to analyze. It allows to study simultaneously all likely hypothesis and verify them with all the available information simultaneously. The outcome will be a table including the evidence and the hypotheses and the results of the evaluation performed (**Table 2**).

In this evaluation, the level correlation is showed:

(+) the evidence supports the hypothesis.

(++) the evidence highly supports the hypothesis.

(−) the evidence does not support the hypothesis.

(−−) the evidence does not support the hypothesis strongly.

Categories	Dimensions
Intrinsic	Accuracy, believability, objectivity, and reputation
Contextual	Value-added, relevancy, timeliness, completeness, and amount of data
Representational	Interpretability, ease of understanding, representational consistency and representation conciseness
Accessibility	Access and security

Table 1.
MIT information quality categories and dimensions (designed by the author, adapted from [15]).

	Hypothesis 1	Hypothesis 2
Evidence	+	+
Evidence	++	—
Evidence	+	Not apply
Evidence	Not apply	—
Evidence	—	+
Total	4+, 1- = 3+	2+, 3- = −1

Table 2.
Resulting table as consequence of the execution of the competing hypothesis method (designed by the author, adapted from [16]).

Not apply: there is no relation between the hypothesis and the evidence.

The winning hypothesis, in the **Table 2** example will be the hypotheses 1, is according to Heuer [16]: "The result of the methodology is which hypothesis has more support according to with the available evidence and not which is the hypothesis with a higher probability of occurrence."

This next to the last step will allow taking the publications selected in the structured searches after the quality evaluation and considering them as the evidence for this method. The hypotheses will be elaborated considering the objective of the systemic method along with the research questions.

This step will identify the winning hypothesis, which means the solution to the problem with more support in the available information.

3.5 Gantt chart

Now that the solution has been found, it is time to design its implementation. To do it, the Gantt chart will be used as method.

To design a Gantt chart, identify objectives and tasks for each implementation phase: design, planning, execution and evaluation.

The objectives preferable must be SMART, which means:

S: Specific, what do you want to achieve? Who needs to participate? When do you want to accomplish your objective? Why is it important?

M: measurable, how can the be progress measured? How do you know if the objective has been achieved?

A: Attainable or Achievable, can you achieve the objective? Do you have the skills needed to achieve the objective? If not, could you build them?

R: Relevant, why it is important? The impact?

T: Timely (or time-bound), when the objective must be accomplished? Is it possible?

George T. Doran coined the concept of SMART objectives, and he published them in the November 1981 issue of Management Review [17]. Since then, some authors added more letters to the acronym, and others created different ones. Still, the general concept remains the same: the objectives gain meaning when a task to be performed is associated to them.

In this final step of the problem-solving tool, the first step is to go back to the systemic method and use it as starting point. Over this scenario, the diagnosis will be performed, but also considering the winning hypotheses from the previous method applied. Considering this information, the specific objectives, and tasks (including the intended duration) must be identified. At this point, a qualitative evaluation is recommended. Asking the people involved in the project for their opinions and suggestions could bring relevant information to the objectives and tasks design for the whole project.

Next to the diagnosis, the planning of what needs to be done is the next stage. It is critical to carefully plan and link the objectives and tasks from this planning stage to the ones in the implementation or execution phase. One of the most common errors is to plan activities that have no correlation on the execution phase or design activities not planned in advance. And also, to put both phases in parallel, when they must be one after the other, sequentially.

Finally, the evaluation phase, it is time to measure if what was implemented has led to the desired scenario or to another. At this point, a qualitative evaluation is recommended.

4. Executing the tool

When we initiate the course discussing the mental models, the participants think about how they see the world and why we all have different opinions. Also, they usually increase their awareness about how bias they are because of their high engagement with the situation they are trying to improve.

It is like they experience Eureka moments.

After this, they can reduce the tension associated with the analysis of the situation and how they consider the other people. This is a first step that facilitates the following ones, when they apply the different methodologies to their problem.

Using the systemic thinking to conceptualize the situation or problem the participants are trying to solve is the next step. This stage is time and energy consuming since a lot of self-questioning and reflection upon not only the scenario but its components, relationships, inputs and outputs and understanding the objective of the system.

Often the participants think they have a problem, but after this phase of deep analysis, they discover sometimes that they were right and in others that it was not the case.

Forcing the participants to prepare the systemic method diagrams, helps them to visualize clearly the situation and they get ready for the next step, which is finding a solution.

Looking for answers and solutions in a structured way is what the participants to this course do when executing the mapping studies.

When performing this task, they complaint a lot because of the effort it takes, but later they realize how important is to have an Excel file that acts as database which condenses all the information.

The link between this method and the systemic thinking is given by the objective of the system which becomes the main research question in the structured search. Using this main question as cornerstone, the relevant aspects to it (and to find answers to the problem) can be easily identified.

Once the relevant publications are selected, its quality is measured using the information quality method. By doing this, since many options or potentials solutions are now identified, this evaluation could be a way to consider which of the available answers have better support.

Competing hypothesis method uses as evidences the publications obtained during the structured search, that also has been evaluated to measure their quality, and ranked. The hypotheses are related to both the objective of the systemic method and the research questions of the mapping. The winning hypotheses, since sets of hypotheses linked to the different aspects of the problem are expected, will be the ones considered to design the implementation plan using the Gantt chart.

The different phases of the Gantt chart, diagnosis, planning, execution and evaluation are developed following the objective of the system (3.1), as guidance, and using winning hypotheses (3.4) as clues to internally organize what must be done to solve the components or aspects of the main problem.

Using this tool, participant to the course solved and implemented problems related to the administrative functioning of a workplace; design new regulations; design and implement customer care systems, etc.

5. Conclusions

This problem-solving course has been presented in different formats over a dozen times, always successfully. A previous publication summarizes the accomplishments until 2016 [18], which were largely surpassed with the new editions of the course and the new venues where it was taught.

Considering the audience and their specific needs, the focus on the different methodologies changes. Usually, the most demanding stage is the implementation of the systemic method in order to conceptualize the problem and also the Gantt design.

The problems that were considered during the courses range from improving to make significant changes. Often, the students implemented what they design during the course, and the results were the ones expected. The effectiveness of this method is proved.

The methodologies included led to finding the solution to many problems, in an unbiased, structured, auditable and at the same time, simple way.

Finally, I consider there is still room for improvements, and maybe shortly more methods or resources will be added to have a more usable and easier to implement tool. Those that are under evaluation are the formal incorporation at the beginning of the curse of an introduction to different decision-making models so the participants would have more information to be applied not only during the problem conceptualisation phase but also to use them at the time of communicating and implemented the solutions. Other resource under evaluation to be added after the Gantt chart is the elaboration of dashboards, which will be useful to monitor the different processes under implementation.

References

[1] ASG – Excellence Through Quality. https://asq.org/quality-resources/problem-solving [Accessed date: 31 October 2021]

[2] Nakagawa T. Creative Problem-Solving Methodologies TRIZ/USIT: Overview of My 14 Years in Research, Education, and Promotion. The Bulletin of the Cultural and Natural Sciences in Osaka Gakuin University, No. 64, March 2012. Available from: http://www.ogjc.osaka-gu.ac.jp/php/nakagawa/TRIZ/eTRIZ/epapers/e2012Papers/eNaka-Overview-1203/eNaka-Overview-120322.pdf [Accessed date: 31 October 2021]

[3] Douglas A, Middleton S, Antony J, Coleman S. Enhancing the Six Sigma problem-solving methodology using the systems thinking methodologies. International Journal of Six Sigma and Competitive Advantage. 2009;**5**(2):144. DOI: 10.1504/ijssca.2009.025166

[4] Richter J, Basten D. Applications of the Viable Systems Model in is Research - A Comprehensive Overview and Analysis, 2014 47th Hawaii International Conference on System Sciences. Waikoloa, HI, USA: IEEE Institute of Electrical and Electronics Engineers; 2014. pp. 4589-4598. DOI: 10.1109/HICSS.2014.565

[5] Newton P. Top 5 Problem Solving Tools, www.free-management-ebooks.com. Available from: http://www.free-management-ebooks.com/dldebk/dlth-5probsolving.htm [Accessed date: 31 October 2021]

[6] University of Arkansas at Pine Bluff, The Six Step Problem Solving Model. Available from: https://www.uapb.edu/sites/www/Uploads/Assessment/webinar/session%203/NewFolder/6%20Step%20Problem%20Solving%20Process.pdf [Accessed date: 31 October 2021]

[7] Beaubien R, Parrish S. The Great Mental Models Volume 1: General Thinking Concepts. Ottawa: Latticework Publishing Inc.; 2018. 190 pag

[8] Wealth TE. The Whole Is Greater Than the Sum of Its Parts. Strategies Newsletter 2012. Available from: https://www.tewealth.com/the-whole-is-greater-than-the-sum-of-its-parts/ [Accessed date: 31 October 2021]

[9] Von Bertalanffy L. General Systems Theory: Foundations, Development and Applications; 1969, 289 pags. Available from: http://monoskop.org/images/7/77/Von_Bertalanffy_Ludwig_General_System_Theory_1968.pdf [Accessed date: 10 August 2021]

[10] Definition of Ecosystem, Encyclopaedia Britannica. Available from: https://www.britannica.com/science/ecosystem [Accessed date: 10 August 2021]

[11] Grant MJ, Booth A. A typology of reviews: An analysis of 14 review types and associated methodologies. Health Information and Libraries Journal. 2009;**26**(2):91-108

[12] Kitchencham B, Pretorius R, Budgen D, Brereton P, Turner M, Niazi M, et al. Guidelines for performing Systematic Literature Reviews in Software Engineering. Information and Software Technology. 2010;**52**:792-805

[13] Genero M, Cruz-Lemus JA, Piattini M. Métodos de investigación en ingeniería del software. Madrid: RaMa; 2014. 312 pag. ISBN 978-84-9964-507-0

[14] Espona MJ, Fisher YC. Teaching information quality to professionals in intelligence government agencies. In: Proceedings of the 32th Information Systems Education Conference

(ISECON). Orlando (Florida, United States): Foundation for IT Education; 2015

[15] Wang RY, Strong D. Beyond accuracy: What data quality means to data consumers. Journal of Management Information Systems. 1996;**12**(4):5-34

[16] Heuer R. Psychology of Intelligence Analysis. Washington, D.C.: Center for the Study of Intelligence; 1999. Available from: https://www.ialeia.org/docs/Psychology_of_Intelligence_Analysis.pdf [Accessed date: 15 August 2021)

[17] Doran GT. There's a S.M.A.R.T. way to write management's goals and objectives. Management Review. 1981;**70**(11):35-36. Available from: https://es.scribd.com/document/458234239/There-s-a-S-M-A-R-T-way-to-write-management-s-goals-and-objectives-George-T-Doran-Management-Review-1981-pdf [Accessed date: 16 August 2021]

[18] Espona MJ. Interdisciplinary integrated tools to problem solving: A short course. US-China education review a. 2016;**6**(11):633-641. DOI: 10.17265/2161-623X/2016.11.002

Index